INSTANT POT COOKBOOK

Lisa Olson

Copyright © 2017

GeorgeSon Press | All Rights Reserved

All rights reserved. No part of this book may be reproduced or transmitted in any form or by any means, electronic or mechanical, including photocopying, recording or by any information storage and retrieval system, without written permission from the publisher, except for the inclusion of brief quotations in a review.

Warning-Disclaimer

The purpose of this book is to educate and entertain. The author or publisher does not guarantee that anyone following the directions, suggestions, tips, ideas, or strategies will achieve the same results. The author and publisher shall have neither liability or responsibility to anyone with respect to any loss or damage caused, or alleged to be caused, directly or indirectly by the information contained in this book.

CONTENTS

Introduction — 6
Getting to Know Your Electric Pressure Cooker — 7
Cooking All-Star Dishes in the Instant Pot — 11
The Surprising Benefits of an Instant Pot — 12
Tips for Using this Recipe Collection –
A New Approach to Cooking — 14
Instant Pot Cooking Time Chart — 15

Vegetables and Side Dishes — 20
1. Hearty Spanish-Style Vegetable Soup — 21
2. Easy Tangy Braised Cabbage — 22
3. Artichokes with Basil Mayonnaise Sauce — 23
4. Winter Sweet Potato and Brown Lentil Soup — 24
5. Garlic and Parsley Mashed Potatoes — 25
6. Hearty Chickpea Stew with Mushrooms — 26
7. Colby Peppery Frittata — 27
8. Spring Veggies with Steamed Eggs — 28
9. One Pot Mushroom Risotto — 29
10. Caramelized Vidalia Onion Soup — 30
11. Creamed Cauliflower Soup with Toasted Garlic — 31
12. Crave-worthy Aromatic Potato Soup — 32
13. Hearty Vegetables with Wheat Berries — 33
14. Yellow Wax Bean Casserole — 34
15. Maple and Balsamic Sweet Potato Mash — 35

Chicken Recipes — 36
16. Zesty Chicken with Apricot Sauce — 37
17. Orange Marmalade-Glazed Chicken Thighs — 38
18. Winter Spicy Chicken Soup — 39
19. Loaded Chicken Sausage Pilaf — 40
20. Green Bean, Snap Pea and Chicken Soup — 41
21. Saucy Sage Chicken Legs — 42
22. Harvest Chicken Stew with Sweet Potatoes — 43
23. Easy Chicken Basmati Risotto — 44
24. Creamy Fettuccine with Chicken and Mushrooms — 45
25. Super Cheesy Chicken Parmesan — 46
26. Mexican-Style Chicken Chili — 47
27. Autumn Chicken and Cauliflower Soup — 48
28. Romano Meatballs in Cheesy Sauce — 49
29. Hot Paprika Wings with Sesame Green Beans — 50
30. Asian-Style Curry and Tomato Chicken — 51

Turkey Recipes — 52
31. Old-Fashioned Turkey with Kidney Beans — 53
32. Mustard Turkey Breasts with Herb Gravy — 54
33. Turkey Sausage with Creamy Broccoli — 55
34. Curried Turkey and Okra Soup — 56
35. Thanksgiving Classic Turkey with Gravy — 57
36. Country-Style Ground Turkey Stew with Noodles — 58
37. Smoked Barbecue Turkey Meatloaf — 59
38. One-Pot Spaghetti and Turkey Meatballs — 60
39. Turkey Drumsticks with Vermouth Pan Sauce — 61
40. Nana's Famous Turkey Corn Chili — 62
41. Holiday Balsamic Turkey Drumettes — 63
42. Turkey Chorizo and Spinach Soup — 64
43. Turkey Chowder with Sweet Peas — 65
44. Easiest Turkey Breast Tenderloin Ever — 66
45. Sinfully Delicious Turkey Risotto — 67

Pork Recipes — 68

46. Perfect Moist and Tender Pulled Pork — 69
47. Breakfast Sausage with Tomato and Chili Chutney — 70
48. Pork-Filled Wontons with Wine Sauce — 71
49. Country-Style Pork and Porcini Stew — 72
50. Sticky Maple Pork Tenderloin with Apples — 73
51. Mustard Pork Cutlets with Green Onions — 74
52. Beer-Braised Pork Butt — 75
53. Tender Festive Sirloin Steak — 76
54. Italian-Style Pork Rib and Pancetta Soup — 77
55. Whiskey Pork Stew with Green Beans — 78
56. Old-Fashioned Pork Lasagna — 79
57. Pork Chops with Pear and Ginger Sauce — 80
58. Finger Lickin' Pork Roast with Pineapple — 81
59. Grandma's Pork and Sausage Cabbage Rolls — 82
60. Faster-than-Fast-Food Pork Ribs — 83

Beef Recipes — 84

61. Veggie and Ground Beef Chunky Soup — 85
62. Family Favorite Beef Stew with Green Peas — 86
63. Penne with Short Ribs and Tomato Sauce — 87
64. Spicy Southwestern Meatloaf — 88
65. Winter Pot Roast with Root Vegetables — 89
66. Mouth-Watering Chipolata Sausage Casserole — 90
67. Braised Beef Shank with Vegetables — 91
68. Beer and Sage Beef Brisket — 92
69. Holiday Cajun Prime Rib — 93
70. Beef and Black Bean Chili with Cilantro Cream — 94
71. Beef and Locatelli Meatballs in Tomato Sauce — 95
72. Festive Tangy and Spicy Beef Salad — 96
73. Split Pea and Ground Beef Soup — 97
74. Colorful Vegetable and Burger Soup — 98
75. Mom's Saucy Chipotle Skirt Steak — 99

Fish & Seafood — 100

76. Everyday Shrimp Pilaf with Parmigiano-Reggiano — 101
77. Cheesy Salmon Pasta Bake — 102
78. Shrimp and Bacon with Apples — 103
79. Chunky Snapper and Vegetable Soup — 104
80. The Easiest Fish Chowder Ever — 105
81. Halibut Steak in Olive-Tomato Sauce — 106
82. Spicy Andouille and Mussel Chowder — 107
83. Kid-Friendly Tuna Salad To-Go — 108
84. Haddock Fillets with Paprika and Mustard Sauce — 109
85. Rich Vegetable and Seafood Risotto — 110
86. Mahi-Mahi with Lima Beans — 111
87. Classic Seafood Lentil Gumbo — 112
88. Easy Creole Butter Haddock — 113
89. Holiday Seafood and Corn Stew — 114
90. Saucy Cod Fillets with Cherry Tomatoes — 115

Vegan Recipes — 116

91. Spicy Garden Vegetable Soup — 117
92. Turnip and Pea Stew — 118
93. Aromatic Basmati Rice with Roasted Peanuts — 119
94. Rustic Potato and Roasted Pepper Soup — 120
95. Spring Risotto with Spinach and Walnuts — 121
96. Vegan Apple Pie Oatmeal — 122
97. Curry Coconut Sweet Potato-Apple Soup — 123
98. Cranberry Pear Breakfast Risotto — 124
99. Easiest Mediterranean Baked Potatoes Ever — 125
100. Vidalia and Sweet Potatoes with Dijon Sauce — 126

101. Steamed Green Beans in Garlic Sauce	127
102. Mom's Saucy Pasta with Cauliflower	128
103. All-In-One Pot Summer Cabbage	129
104. Favorite Wheat Berries with Sautéed Vegetables	130
105. Thai-Style Sweet Corn Soup	131

Snacks & Appetizers 132

106. Corn with Cotija Cheese and Hungarian Paprika	133
107. Garlicky Sautéed Mustard Greens	134
108. Party Marinated Chicken Thighs	135
109. Lamb and Feta Cocktail Meatballs	136
110. Rich Potato Appetizer Salad	137
111. Maple and Sage Carrot Sticks	138
112. Crispy Herby Sweet Potato Balls	139
113. Orange Glazed Chicken Drumettes	140
114. Nutty and Yummy Beet Appetizer	141
115. Buttery Marjoram Fingerling Potatoes	142
116. Zingy Parsnip Bites	143
117. Artichokes with Spicy Mayonnaise Sauce	144
118. Eggplant and Pepper Dipping Sauce	145
119. Must-Serve Stuffed Eggs	146
120. Spicy Sausage and Tomato Dip	147

Beans & Grains 148

121. Turkey Chipotle Chili with Scallions	149
122. Congee with Sesame and Vegetables	150
123. Homemade Paprika Cheddar Cornbread	151
124. Cajun Sausage Oatmeal	152
125. Autumn Apple and Walnut Couscous	153
126. Herbed Sausage and Scallion Grits	154
127. Cheesy Truffled Oatmeal with Mushrooms	155
128. Two-Bean Everyday Chili	156
129. Vegan Holiday Black-Eyed Peas	157
130. Sausage Pilaf with Herbs and Almonds	158
131. Herby Polenta Bowl with Prosciutto	159
132. Fancy Mixed Berry Porridge	160
133. Kale, Ham Hock and Bean Soup	161
134. Pizza-Style Baked Beans	162
135. Herby Polenta Squares with Parmesan	163

Dessert Recipes 164

136. Date-Vanilla Ciabatta Bread Pudding	165
137. Cranberry and Pecan Zucchini Bread	166
138. Festive Dried Fruit and Walnut Pudding	167
139. Holiday Orange and Raspberry Cheesecake	168
140. Maple and Fig Yogurt Dessert	169
141. Peach and Raspberry Crumble	170
142. Nana's Famous Walnut Fudge Brownies	171
143. Extravagant Currant Rice Pudding	172
144. Aromatic Wine-Poached Apples	173
145. Luscious Key Blueberry Delight	174
146. Decadent Mint Cheesecake	175
147. Every-Day Banana Bread Muffins	176
148. Triple Chocolate Fudge Cake	177
149. Elegant Creamy Tropical Dessert	178
150. Berry and Prune Compote	179

INTRODUCTION

If you thought pressure cookers were a clumsy cookware and an item of the past, nothing could be further from the truth! Today, this amazing kitchen appliance is making a comeback and, whether you're a new beginner or a professional chef, you'll soon find yourself whipping up old-fashioned refried beans, casseroles, soups, stews, etc. As a matter of fact, modern pressure cooking today is a stunning "union" of traditional cooking techniques and high-tech kitchen gadgets. Welcome to the world of pressure cooker renaissance! Welcome to one-pot meals!

GETTING TO KNOW YOUR ELECTRIC PRESSURE COOKER

Coming home to a homemade meal is the perfect end of a busy and stressful day. However, most of us don't have hours to spend in the kitchen and we often feel overwhelmed; on the other hand, we tend to minimize our bakeware and cookware. In other words, we don't want to slave over a hot stove; thus, we are constantly looking for kitchen appliances that make cooking easier and more comfortable.

Instant Pot is a super-sophisticated machine that utilizes high pressure to speed up the cooking time of your favorite food; it cooks your food as much as 70 percent faster than regular stove-top method. If you have ever had a hard time cooking for family gatherings and holidays, you know how much it matters to you. This cooker helps you cook an entire meal at once. You can make whole roasted chicken, homey stews, the best corn-on-the-cob, hearty meatloaf, puffy bread, delectable cake, and other comfort food in one pot. It is a perfect kitchen companion for food-centric holidays such as Christmas and Thanksgiving Day. Much less mess and stress! Furthermore, cooking in a pressurized environment allows you to make healthier food choices because your food retains its valuable nutrients. The amazing aromas and flavors are more concentrated too. Thus, if you choose a pressure cooking, you are choosing one of the healthiest ways to meet your nutritional requirements. Best of all, the Instant Pot saves your money by cooking inexpensive ingredients in bulk. You simply utilize an automated cooking process and hyper-pressurized environment to improve your health, as well as save your precious time and hard-earned money!

The Instant Pot is a multifunctional programmable cooker that offers a wide variety of delicious homemade meals. It can do the job of a sauté pan, electric pressure cooker, slow cooker, rice and porridge maker, steamer, warming pot, and yogurt maker. Incredible!

Here are the major points you need to know for getting the most out of your Instant Pot.

1. How does the Instant Pot electric pressure cooker work – the quick facts.

- First things first: read the manual carefully before you start using your new device.

- Briefly, an air-tight lid locks into place. Cooking liquids come to a boil under a sealed lid and they transform to a steam shortly thereafter. This winning combination of the super-heated steam and "trapped" pressure begins to cook food more quickly than traditional appliances.

- When it comes to the cook times, it takes from 10 to 13 minutes to get up to pressure and about 15 to 20 minutes to release the pressure completely before removing the lid.

- If you tend to convert conventional pressure cooker recipes into the Instant Pot recipes, it is good to know that the Instant Pot operates at 11.5 PSI; therefore, it takes longer to cook than a stovetop pressure cooker. However, please consult the chart below for the proper cooking time.

- This is an intelligent, programmable multi-cooker, which means you can set up your Instant Pot to 24-hours in advance.

- If you're just getting started with your Instant Pot, it may seem complicated. But once you understand the basics of pressure cooking, this opens up new possibilities to make the best family meals ever! You plug it in, place the ingredients, choose the function, and let it go. Obviously, with a great cookware and a dash of cleverness, anyone can become a good home cook!

- At first glance, you will notice a control panel with a lot of buttons. There's no need to panic because almost all these buttons cook the same way; in fact, they have different cooking times programmed for different food types and that's all! After all, you can always use the "Manual" button i.e. "+" and "-" buttons to adjust the cooking time.

- Then, for the vast majority of recipes we use High pressure; actually, this is default setting on the Instant Pot. Delicate foods such as eggs cook on a low-pressure setting, which is rarely used.

2. Instant Pot smart cooking programs

With all of that in mind, it's time to use this revolutionary one-touch technology. All you have to do is choose one of the pre-set buttons. But which one?

MANUAL button is the most common; you can adjust the time and temperature according to your unique recipe and your personal preferences. Think of it as an all-purpose button.

MULTIGRAIN – use this function to cook rice and grains quickly and effortlessly. Make sure to check cooking time charts before pressure cooking.

SOUP – this is a great program designed for homemade soups, stocks and chowders. It uses High pressure and 30-minute cook time by default; of course, you are able to increase and decrease cook time. This program cooks your soup perfectly without boiling too heavily.

PORRIDGE – fully automated function for rice porridge, as well as for a mixture of different grains.

RICE – use this function specifically for cooking different types of rice at Low pressure. Cooking duration depends on the food amount. For instance, it takes about 13 minutes to cook 2 cups of rice. For more than 2 cups, it takes approximately 26 minutes.

YOGURT – this is two-step program designed for making a homemade healthy yogurt. You will be able to make yogurt in individual glass canning jars too!

POULTRY – this program is perfect for making a bird with crispy skin and flavorful, juicy meat.

MEAT/STEW – an automated function for making budget-friendly and great-tasting meat recipes at High pressure. Cooking duration depends on a type of meat you use.

BEAN/CHILI – an excellent program for dry, soaked and canned beans. However, don't forget to consult cooking time charts.

STEAM – as the name says, you prepare your food by the application of steam. You should use cooking utensils such as a metal steam rack or steamer basket. Finally, you get an intensely flavorful food with maximum taste and color.

SLOW COOK – this program is very economical to use because it is great for cooking cheaper cuts and root vegetables. It is an excellent choice for busy households and for everyone who wants a meal ready when they arrive home.

SAUTÉ – this function allows you to brown the meat and sweat vegetables prior to cooking. This step takes a little time and effort but it will significantly enhance the flavors. Remove the cooker's lid when using this function.

KEEP WARM/CANCEL – to turn off the cooker and time the meals. Once pressure cooking is done, press the "Cancel" button; otherwise, the warming function is automatically activated.

3. A Natural release or Quick release

In terms of the Natural pressure release method, simply press the "Cancel" button or unplug it, and let your cooker stand until the float valve sinks. Finally, wait for about 10 minutes before releasing any remaining pressure.

If you want to stop the pressure cooking quickly and release the steam manually, use the Quick pressure release. And remember – keep your hands away from the steam as it's released!

COOKING ALL-STAR DISHES IN THE INSTANT POT

Some of your favorite family recipes can turn out really delicious and moist in the Instant Pot. However, here are a few major points to keep in mind for the best results.

- Vegetables are one of the best ingredients to cook in your electric pressure cooker. It is important to wash all vegetables and dry them in the usual way. In addition, you can cook them directly from the frozen state! It's recommended to use "Steam" function to preserve nutrients. It is the ideal cooking method for the tough, flowery vegetables such as artichokes.

- When it comes to the Instant Pot soups, your machine can sauté veggies, simmer a liquid, and finish a soup without using another pots and pans. Never fill your cooker over three-quarters full; otherwise, there will not be enough room to create the cooking steam.

- The Instant Pot cooks beans and grains super-fast. For the best results, you should soak dried beans before cooking time. To cook perfect rice, the best water-to-rice ratio is 1:1, including rinsed wet rice. Cooking times depend on types of rice.

- The Instant Pot transforms the meat into fork-tender delicious bites in record time. When it comes to the cooking times, there are a few factors that may affect it – the type of meat, the size of the meat cut, fresh or frozen state, etc. You can brown the meat to naturally improve the taste of your meals using the "Sauté" function. If you cook meat and vegetables together, it is recommended to use" stop-and-go" cooking and the quick-release method.

THE SURPRISING BENEFITS OF AN INSTANT POT

1. A genius way to eat healthier and lose weight in the process.

"If you don't take care of your body, where are you going to live?" – This is a sentence we've all heard. Nevertheless, most of us are eating fast food on a regular basis, skipping meals with negative consequences, trying to lose weight in many unhealthy ways. In other words, we follow unhealthy lifestyle. Luckily, the solution is at your fingertips – pressure cooking might help you break the fast food habit in an easy way.

Many studies have shown that pressure cooking tends to preserve nutrients better than steaming, roasting and boiling. The Instant Pot utilizes shorter cooking time and super-heated steam that is very evenly distributed; nutrients are not dispersed to the air because they can't escape from the sealed environment. It helps the ingredients to preserve more of their whole food nutrition. It also requires less oil and water so that vitamins and minerals are not dissolved away by cooking liquid.

Grains and legumes become more digestible in the Instant Pot; pressure cooking reduces phytic acid and lectins (anti-nutrients) in grains. Many studies have proven that pressure cooking increases the digestibility of protein. For example, protein digestibility of pressure-cooking soaked peas is about 84%, which is higher in comparison with peas that are cooked normally.

The same goes for meat; pressure cooking can tenderize any kind of meat and turn tough fibers into gelatin so it is much easier for our stomach to digest. It is great that you can lose weight for the same reason.

A cooking method is very important but the ingredients you use on a daily basis matter a lot. Cooking your own meals in the Instant Pot allows you to have control over what ingredients you use.

This recipe collection is chock-full of inspirational recipes that promote a well-balanced diet for life-long health.

These recipes contain good fats such as butter, coconut oil, and olive oil that can have positive health benefits. These easy-to-follow recipes also include a lot of fruits, vegetables, fish, seafood, fresh herbs, and other healthy ingredients.

2. An incredible way to save time and money when you cook at home.

Choose your food and kitchen equipment wisely and you will save lots of time and money in the long-term. Choose fix-it and forget-it meals with maximum taste and minimal cleanup! The instant pot is the most advanced electric pressure cooker that prepares super-quick, one-pot meals that otherwise would take hours in the kitchen.

From here on out, you can cook an entire meal in your smart electric pressure cooker. For most of the Instant Pot recipes, you don't need other pots, pans, skillets, etc. Except for basic tools and utensils, maybe a blender, you'll be cleaning up just one cooking pot. Great!

The Instant Pot has proven to be the great kitchen tool of those cooks who don't want to spend all day in the kitchen but want to offer flavorful meals to their families.

When it comes to saving money, pressure cookers can tenderize inexpensive cuts of meat and cook budget-friendly dishes like beans, oats, chicken thighs and stocks to perfection. Many of these recipes call for staples you already have in your pantry. When compared to other cooking methods, the Instant Pot uses two to three times less electricity. Therefore, bear in mind that your electric pressure cooker is economical and eco-friendly!

TIPS FOR USING THIS RECIPE COLLECTION — A NEW APPROACH TO COOKING

We have got 150 recipes ahead that will make your pressure cooking experience more enjoyable! The recipes are grouped into 11 different categories so everyone can reap the benefits.

Whether you have just purchased your pressure cooker or you have been using it for years, this recipe collection is ready to be your steady kitchen companion. To make pressure cooking super-easy, every recipe contains the ingredient list, detailed step-by-step instruction, the number of servings, and cooking time. In addition, each and every recipe includes the nutritional information so you will be able to track your intake and consumption. You will find a lot of useful information such as creative serving ideas, food facts and kitchen tips from the best chefs, ingredient substitute ideas, and so on.

You can take some of your favorite pressure cooker recipes and adjust them to be made in the Instant Pot. Converting traditional stovetop recipes into Instant Pot recipes is easy too. However, it takes some patience and practice. Like everything in life, you should have passion for cooking and some experience. In fact, cooking is a lifelong adventure. Once you become familiar with your Instant Pot and its fantastic features, the beautiful adventure begins!

Later, you will be able to adjust cooking times and measurements to fit your preferences and you won't be afraid to experiment with these recipes. The charts below describe specific time adjustments you should follow when cooking in your Instant Pot.

However, the best way to experience the Instant Pot is to cook and try these recipes. Let's move from words to deeds and do not forget to add a heaping spoonful of love!

INSTANT POT COOKING TIME CHART

Please note that cooking times are approximate; use them as a guideline only. These cooking times are for the medium amount of food. In order to cook a large amount of food, you should add more liquid and increase the time by 20-40%.

VEGETABLES	Fresh, Cooking Time in Minutes	Frozen, Cooking Time in Minutes
Artichokes, whole	9 – 11	11 – 13
Artichokes, hearts	4 – 5	5 – 6
Artichokes, baby	4	5 – 6
Asparagus, whole	1 – 2	2 – 3
Beans, green and yellow	1 – 2	2 – 3
Beets, small	11 – 13	13 – 15
Beets, large	20 – 25	25 – 30
Bok Choy	5-7	7-8
Broccoli, flowerets	2 – 3	3 – 4
Broccoli, stalks	3 – 4	4 – 5
Brussel sprouts	3 – 4	4 – 5
Cabbage, red, purple or green	2 – 3	3 – 4
Carrots, slices	1 – 2	2 – 3
Carrots, whole	2 – 3	3 – 4
Cauliflower, flowerets	2 – 3	3 – 4
Cauliflower, whole	8	8-10
Celery, slices	2 – 3	3 – 4
Chard, Swiss	5	5-7
Chinese cabbage	5	5-7
Collard	4 – 5	5 – 6
Corn, kernels	1 – 2	2 – 3
Corn, on the cob	3 – 4	4 – 5
Eggplant, slices	2 – 3	3 – 4
Endive	1 – 2	2 – 3
Escarole	1 – 2	2 – 3
Leafy greens	3 – 6	4 – 7
Leeks	2 – 4	3 – 5
Mushrooms, dry	10	N/A
Mushrooms, fresh	5	5-7

Okra	2 – 3	3 – 4
Onions	2 – 3	3 – 4
Parsnips	1 – 2	2 – 3
Peas	1 – 2	2 – 3
Potatoes, cubes	7 – 9	9 – 11
Potatoes, whole	12 – 15	15 – 19
Potatoes, baby	10 – 12	12 – 14
Pumpkin, small slices	4 – 5	6 – 7
Pumpkin, large slices	8 – 10	10 – 14
Rutabaga, sliced	3 – 5	4 – 6
Spinach	1 – 2	3 – 4
Squash, acorn	6 – 7	8 – 9
Squash, butternut	8 – 10	10 – 12
Sweet potato, cubes	7 – 9	9 – 11
Sweet potato, small	10 – 12	12 – 14
Sweet potato, large	12 – 15	15 – 19
Sweet pepper, slices	1 – 3	2 – 4
Tomatoes, quartered	2 – 3	4 – 5
Tomatoes, whole	3 – 5	5 – 7
Turnip	2 – 4	4 – 6
Yam, cubes	7 – 9	9 – 11
Yam, small	10 – 12	12 – 14
Yam, large	12 – 15	15 – 19
Zucchini	2 – 3	3 – 4

RICE & GRAINS	Water Quantity (Grain : Water ratio)	Cooking Time in Minutes
Barley, pearl	1:4	25 – 30
Congee, thick	1:4 ~ 1:5	15 – 20
Congee, thin	1:6 ~ 1:7	15 – 20
Couscous	1:2	5 – 8
Corn, dried	1:3	25 – 30
Kamut, whole	1:3	10 – 12
Millet	1:1 2/3	10 – 12
Oats, quick cooking	1:1 2/3	6
Oats, steel-cut	1:1 2/3	10
Porridge, thin	1:6 ~ 1:7	15 – 20
Quinoa, quick cooking	1:2	8
Rice, Basmati	1: 1.5	4 – 8

Rice, Brown	1: 1.25	22 – 28
Rice, Jasmine	1: 1	4 – 10
Rice, white	1: 1.5	8
Rice, wild	1:3	25 – 30
Sorghum	1:3	20 – 25
Spelt berries	1:3	15 – 20
Wheat berries	1:3	25 – 30

BEANS, LEGUMES & LENTILS	Dry, Cooking Time in Minutes	Soaked, Cooking Time in Minutes
Adzuki	20 – 25	10 – 15
Anasazi	20 – 25	10 – 15
Black beans	20 – 25	10 – 15
Black-eyed peas	20 – 25	10 – 15
Chickpeas	35 – 40	20 – 25
Cannellini beans	35 – 40	20 – 25
Gandules	20 – 25	15 – 20
Great Northern beans	25 – 30	20 – 25
Lentils, French green	15 – 20	N/A
Lentils, green and brown	15 – 20	N/A
Lentils, red and split	15 – 18	N/A
Lentils (moong dal)	15 – 18	N/A
Lima beans	20 – 25	10 – 15
Kidney beans, red	25 – 30	20 – 25
Kidney beans, white	35 – 40	20 – 25
Navy beans	25 – 30	20 – 25
Pinto beans	25 – 30	20 – 25
Peas	15 – 20	10 – 15
Soy beans	25 – 30	20 – 25

MEAT	Cooking Time in Minutes
Beef, brisket	70
Beef, dressed	20 – 25
Beef, flank steak	15
Beef, ground	6
Beef, pot roast, steak, rump, round (large)	35 – 40
Beef, pot roast, steak, rump (chunks)	25 – 30
Beef, ribs	60
Beef, shanks	25 – 30

Beef, stew (cubes)	12
Beef, stock	60
Beef, tongue	50
Beef, oxtail	40 – 50
Chicken, breasts	8 – 10
Chicken, drumsticks and thighs	10 – 15
Chicken, ground	5
Chicken, liver	3
Chicken, stock (bones, etc.)	35
Chicken, strips	1
Chicken, whole (up to 4lbs)	20 – 25
Cornish Hen, whole	10 – 15
Duck, cut up with bones	10 – 12
Duck, whole	25 – 30
Goat	20
Goose, pieces	20
Ham, slices	9 – 12
Ham picnic shoulder	25 – 30
Hare	35
Lamb, cubes	10 – 15
Lamb, ground	12
Lamb, leg/shank	35 – 45
Lamb, roast	20
Lamb, shoulder	25
Lamb, stew meat	10 – 15
Pheasant	20 – 25
Pigeon	25
Pork, belly	40
Pork, butt roast	45 – 50
Pork, ground	5
Pork, leg/shank	35
Pork, loin	12
Pork, ribs	20 – 25
Pork, roast	30
Pork sausage	8
Pork, shoulder	50
Pork, stew (cubed)	8
Pork, stock (bones, etc.)	60
Quail	9
Rabbit	18
Turkey, breast, boneless	15 – 20
Turkey, breast, whole, with bones	25 – 30
Turkey, drumsticks	15 – 20
Turkey, wings	20
Veal, chops	5 – 8

Veal, ground	6
Veal, Osso buco	20
Veal, roast	35 – 45
Veal, stock (bones, etc.)	60
Veal, tongue	40

FISH & SEAFOOD	Fresh, Cooking Time in Minutes	Frozen, Cooking Time in Minutes
Crab	3 – 4	5 – 6
Fish fillet	2 – 3	3 – 4
Fish steak	3 – 4	4 – 6
Lobster	3 – 4	4 – 6
Mussels	2 – 3	4 – 5
Seafood soup or stock	6 – 7	7 – 9
Shrimp	1 – 2	2 – 3
Snapper, whole	5 – 6	7 – 10
Trout, whole	5 – 6	7 – 10

FRUITS	Fresh, Cooking Time in Minutes	Dried, Cooking Time in Minutes
Apples, slices	2 – 3	3 – 4
Apples, whole	3 – 4	4 – 6
Apricots	2 – 3	3 – 4
Peaches	2 – 3	4 – 5
Pears, slices	2 – 3	4 – 5
Pears, whole	3 – 4	4 – 6
Prunes	2 – 3	4 – 5
Raisins	N/A	4 – 5

VEGETABLES AND SIDE DISHES

2

5

8

11

14

1. Hearty Spanish-Style Vegetable Soup

 6 Servings

 Ready in about 15 minutes

PER SERVING:
358 Calories; 3.6g Fat; 64.6g Carbs; 20.5g Protein; 10.6g Sugars

White beans like Great Northern or Navy beans work great for this recipe but you can freely use any kind of kidney beans. Keep in mind that your cooker reaches the temperature and pressure depending on the temperature of your vegetables, i.e. whether or not they are frozen.

INGREDIENTS

- 1 tablespoon olive oil
- 1 onion, chopped
- 2 garlic cloves, pressed
- 3 large-sized carrots, cleaned, trimmed and sliced
- 1 head cauliflower, chopped into florets
- 3/4 (15-ounce) can tomatoes with juice, diced
- 2 (15-ounce) cans white beans with juice
- 1/4 cup quinoa, rinsed
- 1/4 cup tomato paste
- 1 tablespoon hot sauce
- 1 teaspoon cumin powder
- 1 teaspoon cayenne pepper
- 2 bay leaves
- 3/4 teaspoon fine sea salt
- 1/2 teaspoon freshly cracked black peppercorns
- 2 ½ cups boiling vegetable stock

COOKING STEPS

1. Simply place all of the above ingredients into your Instant Pot. Give it a good stir and lock the lid into place.

2. Now, press the "Manual" button; select HIGH pressure and 2-minutes cooking time.

3. Finally, press the "Cancel" button and use a quick release; carefully remove the cover. Discard the bay leaves and serve in individual bowls. Bon appétit!

2. EASY TANGY BRAISED CABBAGE

 4 Servings

 Ready in about 25 minutes

PER SERVING:
151 Calories; 4.1g Fat; 27.0g Carbs; 5.2g Protein; 13.4g Sugars

Juicy, tangy cabbage that is lightly seasoned and pressure cooked. This recipe can be served as a side dish or a vegetarian main course; however, this is the meal that your family will love for sure!

INGREDIENTS

- 1 tablespoon olive oil
- 1 onion, cut into wedges
- 1 medium-sized cabbage, cut into wedges
- 1 celery stalk, grated
- 1 carrot, grated
- 1 ¼ cups vegetable stock
- 1/4 cup balsamic vinegar
- 1 teaspoon garlic powder
- 1/2 teaspoon paprika
- 1/2 teaspoon salt
- 1/2 teaspoon ground black pepper
- 1 tablespoon cornstarch

COOKING STEPS

1. Choose "Sauté" mode to preheat your cooker. Then, warm the olive oil and sauté the onion and cabbage until they're just tender and fragrant.

2. Add the remaining ingredients without the cornstarch, and gently stir to combine. Set the timer for 5 minutes and cook at HIGH pressure.

3. Once pressure cooking is complete, use a normal release (it will take about 15 minutes). Carefully remove the cover.

4. Discard the vegetables; now, reheat the cooking liquid on "Sauté" mode. Take a mixing bowl and make the slurry by whisking the cornstarch with a tablespoon of water. Add the slurry to the cooker and boil the liquid until it has thickened.

5. Pour this sauce over the veggies and serve warm. Bon appétit!

3. ARTICHOKES WITH BASIL MAYONNAISE SAUCE

 4 Servings

 Ready in about 30 minutes

PER SERVING:
151 Calories; 4.1g Fat; 27.0g Carbs; 5.2g Protein; 13.4g Sugars

For this recipe, select the artichokes with closed petals. In that way, your pressure-cooked artichokes will be more tender and tastier. Artichokes are packed with antioxidants, vitamins, and dietary fiber.

INGREDIENTS

- 2 artichokes, trimmed
- 2 tablespoons of lemon juice
- 1 tablespoon chopped fresh basil
- 4 tablespoons mayonnaise
- Salt and black pepper, to taste
- 1 teaspoon whole-grain mustard
- 1 teaspoon cayenne pepper

COOKING STEPS

1. Drizzle the artichokes with lemon juice. Pour 1 cup of water into the Instant Pot base; add a steamer basket. Lay the artichokes in the basket.

2. Seal the cooker and select "Manual" mode. Cook for 18 to 25 minutes at HIGH pressure.

3. Once cooking is done, perform a natural release.

4. Meanwhile, process the remaining ingredients in a blender or a food processor until everything's well incorporated. Serve with warm artichokes.

4. Winter Sweet Potato and Brown Lentil Soup

 6 Servings

 Ready in about 25 minutes

PER SERVING:
229 Calories; 0.9g Fat; 44.2g Carbs; 12.2g Protein; 3.8g Sugars

Is there anything better than rich warm soup during winter weekdays? Serve warm with rice, pasta, or crusty bread.

INGREDIENTS

- 1 tablespoon olive oil
- 1 medium-sized leek, sliced
- 2 cloves garlic, peeled and pressed
- 1 large-sized carrot, trimmed and chopped
- 1 stalk celery, cleaned and chopped
- 2 small-sized sweet potatoes, peeled and cubed
- 1 teaspoon salt
- Ground black pepper, to your liking
- 1 teaspoon paprika
- 1/4 teaspoon chili powder
- 1 teaspoon coriander, finely minced
- 1 teaspoon fennel seeds
- 2 bay leaves
- 1 ¼ cups brown lentils
- 1 cup water
- 1 cup roasted vegetable stock
- 1 can tomatoes with juices
- 2 tablespoons tomato paste

COOKING STEPS

1. Preheat your Instant Pot by pressing the "Sauté" button; heat the oil. Now, sauté the leeks and garlic until just tender or about 3 minutes.

2. Then, put the carrots, celery, and sweet potatoes in; add all seasonings and stir to combine. Continue to cook for 2 more minutes.

3. Next, add the brown lentils, water, and the stock. Use "Manual" function and 10-minute cooking time. Once cooking is complete, perform a natural release.

4. Carefully and slowly take off the lid; add the canned tomatoes and tomato paste; press the "Sauté" button and cook for 5 more minutes, stirring frequently. Serve over rice. Bon appétit!

5. GARLIC AND PARSLEY MASHED POTATOES

 4 Servings

 Ready in about 20 minutes

PER SERVING:
253 Calories; 9.3g Fat; 37.9g Carbs; 6.1g Protein; 4.5g Sugars

You don't have to heat up your whole stove for just cooking a few potatoes. You can get even better mashed potatoes in your Instant Pot.

INGREDIENTS

- 1/3 cup water
- 4 potatoes, peeled
- 2/3 cup milk
- 3/4 tablespoon butter
- 1/2 cup sour cream
- 2 garlic cloves, minced
- 1/2 teaspoon ground black pepper
- 1 teaspoon garlic salt
- 1 tablespoon fresh parsley, chopped

COOKING STEPS

1. Add the water and potatoes to the Instant Pot; seal the lid.

2. Select "Manual" mode; cook at HIGH pressure for 10 minutes.

3. In the meantime, warm the milk and butter until heated through. Once pressure cooking has completed, use a quick release. Check the potatoes for doneness; drain and reserve a small amount of cooking liquid.

4. Mash your potatoes until all lumps are gone. Add the warm milk mixture and mix thoroughly. Now, add the sour cream, garlic, black pepper, and salt.

5. You can add the cooking liquid if needed and mix to combine well. Serve garnished with fresh parsley.

6. HEARTY CHICKPEA STEW WITH MUSHROOMS

 8 Servings

 Ready in about 15 minutes

PER SERVING:
414 Calories; 18.2g Fat; 50.6 Carbs; 16.2g Protein; 10.8g Sugars

Chickpea is often considered to be a flashy vegetable, but it can add rich flavor and nutrition to any stew recipe. In this vegetarian recipe, canned chickpea cooks with fresh vegetables for just 10 minutes. Serve with pressure cooked mashed potatoes and enjoy!

INGREDIENTS

- 2 tablespoons butter
- 1 yellow onion, finely chopped
- 1 garlic clove, chopped
- 1 cup fresh white mushrooms, sliced
- 1-2 parsnips, trimmed and chopped
- 3 cups canned chickpeas, well drained
- 1 can stewed tomatoes
- 1 ½ cups non-dairy milk
- 1 teaspoon kosher salt
- 1/2 teaspoon mixed peppercorns, freshly cracked
- 1/4 teaspoon smoked cayenne pepper
- 1/4 teaspoon dried or fresh dill weed

COOKING STEPS

1. Firstly, preheat the Instant Pot by selecting the "Sauté" key. Once hot, melt the butter.

2. Now, add the onion, garlic, mushrooms and parsnips; cook until tender or about 4 minutes.

3. After that, put the remaining ingredients in. Secure the lid and use "Soup" function and 10-minute cook time.

4. Once cooking is complete, perform a quick release. Serve warm with mashed potatoes if desired.

7. COLBY PEPPERY FRITTATA

 4 Servings

 Ready in about 40 minutes

PER SERVING:
300 Calories; 23.7g Fat; 7.2g Carbs; 16.2g Protein; 4.4g Sugars

Eggs, peppers and freshly grated cheese are all cooked together in this custardy frittata for an appetizing breakfast. You can substitute Monterey Jack for Colby cheese. Enjoy!

INGREDIENTS

- 1 tablespoon olive oil
- 1 onion, chopped
- 1 red bell pepper, deveined and chopped
- 1 Serrano pepper, deveined and chopped
- 1 ½ cups water
- 4 eggs
- 1 teaspoon multi-grain mustard
- 2 tablespoons sour cream
- 1/4 cup Colby cheese, freshly grated
- 1/2 teaspoon sea salt
- 1/2 teaspoon smoked cayenne pepper
- 1 tablespoon fresh coriander, chopped

COOKING STEPS

1. First warm the oil using "Sauté" button; then, sauté the onions and pepper until just tender and fragrant.

2. Pour the water into the base of your Instant Pot; insert the steam rack on top. Then, take a soufflé dish and spritz it lightly with a non-stick cooking spray.

3. In a mixing dish, whisk the eggs, mustard, and sour cream. Fold in the pepper mixture; add the grated cheese and gently stir to combine. Season with salt, green peppercorns, cayenne pepper, and coriander.

4. Scrape the prepared mixture into the lightly greased soufflé dish. Cover with foil; lower onto the steam rack.

5. Secure the lid; press the "Manual" button and cook for 20 minutes using LOW pressure.

6. Once cooking is complete, use a quick pressure release. Serve on individual plates with some extra sour cream if desired. Bon appétit!

8. SPRING VEGGIES WITH STEAMED EGGS

 2 Servings

 Ready in about 15 minutes

PER SERVING:
131 Calories; 6.1g Fat;
10.7g Carbs; 9.2g Protein;
6.6g Sugars

The combination of the fluffy eggs and fresh green veggies is suitable for brunch, dinner or light spring lunch. Serve with enough English muffins or homemade bread.

INGREDIENTS

- 2 eggs
- 2/3 cup milk
- 1/2 cup spring onions, chopped
- 1 green garlic, chopped
- 1 carrot, finely chopped
- 1/4 teaspoon ground black peppercorns
- Salt and crushed red pepper flakes, to taste

COOKING STEPS

1. Firstly, whisk the eggs with the milk in a small-sized mixing dish or a measuring cup. Transfer the mixture to a heat-proof bowl that is previously lightly greased with a non-stick cooking spray.

2. Mix the spring onions, green garlic, carrot, black peppercorns, salt, and red pepper; gently stir until everything is well incorporated.

3. Pour 1 cup of water into the inner pot of your Instant Pot. Insert the trivet in the Instant Pot. Lower the heat-proof bowl onto the trivet.

4. Close the cooker and close the vent valve. Select "Manual" mode and HIGH pressure; cook for 5 minutes.

5. Afterward, use a quick pressure release. Serve warm with sliced radishes. Bon appétit!

9. ONE POT MUSHROOM RISOTTO

 8 Servings

 Ready in about 40 minutes

PER SERVING:
198 Calories; 1.9g Fat;
39.4g Carbs; 4.4g Protein;
1.2g Sugars

Mushrooms, along with fragrant seasonings, go well with white risotto in every recipe, whatever cooking method you prefer to use. But this risotto is made saucy in no time.

INGREDIENTS

- 1 cup porcini mushrooms, dried
- 4 cups warm water
- 1 tablespoon butter, softened
- 1 onion, chopped
- 2 cups fresh white mushrooms, sliced
- 2 cups white rice
- 2 tablespoons dry white wine
- 1/2 teaspoon turmeric powder
- 1/4 teaspoon smoked cayenne pepper
- 1/2 teaspoon dried dill weed
- Sea salt and freshly cracked black pepper, to taste
- 2 cups roasted vegetable stock
- Fresh chopped chives, for garnish

COOKING STEPS

1. Meanwhile, preheat the cooker using "Sauté" mode; warm the butter, and sauté the onion with the soaked porcini mushrooms and the fresh white mushrooms. Now, cook until the onions are translucent and the mushrooms are just tender and fragrant.

2. Now, put the rice in, the wine, and all the seasonings; cook, stirring continuously, until the liquid has completely evaporated.

3. Pour in the remaining 2 cups of warm water along with the stock. Lock the cooker's lid according to the manual; set the timer for 8 minutes.

4. Afterward, use a quick release and carefully remove the lid. Serve warm garnished with fresh chopped chives. Bon appétit!

10. CARAMELIZED VIDALIA ONION SOUP

 6 Servings

 Ready in about 30 minutes

PER SERVING:
118 Calories; 5.2g Fat; 13.9g Carbs; 1.9g Protein; 7.6g Sugars

Vidalia onions and carefully selected spices are magically transformed into a hearty French-style soup that is healthy as well. In this recipe, you can experiment and substitute the other kinds of sweet onion for Vidalia.

INGREDIENTS

- 2 tablespoons vegetable oil
- 1 ½ pounds Vidalia onions, cut into thinly slices
- 1/4 teaspoon freshly cracked black pepper
- 3/4 teaspoon salt
- 1 tablespoon white sugar
- 1/2 cup dry white wine
- 5 ½ cups vegetable stock
- 1 fresh thyme sprig
- Toasted French bread slices, to serve

COOKING STEPS

1. Preheat your Instant Pot by selecting "Sauté" mode. Then, heat the oil and sauté the Vidalia onions until just tender and translucent; it will take about 5 minutes.

2. After that, add black pepper, salt, and white sugar. Continue cooking, stirring continuously, until the onions are caramelized.

3. Pour in the wine in order to scrape off any brown bits from the bottom of the cooker. Now, add the stock and thyme.

4. Stir, secure the lid, and select "Manual" function; cook at HIGH pressure for 9 minutes. Ladle the soup into individual bowls and serve with toasted French bread.

11. CREAMED CAULIFLOWER SOUP WITH TOASTED GARLIC

 6 Servings

 Ready in about 30 minutes

PER SERVING:
163 Calories; 2.7g Fat; 30.0g Carbs; 6.4g Protein; 4.5g Sugars

Never underestimate the importance of a good healthy soup at lunchtime. Inspired by root vegetables, you can come up with this soup recipe that is just scrumptious!

INGREDIENTS

- 1 tablespoon olive oil, at room temperature
- 2 garlic cloves, thinly sliced
- 1 medium-sized head cauliflower
- 1 carrot, trimmed and chopped
- 4 Russet potatoes, peeled and diced
- 1 parsnip, chopped
- 1 large-sized shallot, peeled and finely chopped
- 1 teaspoon sea salt
- 1/2 teaspoon ground black pepper, or more to taste
- 1/2 teaspoon dried rosemary
- 1/4 teaspoon dried basil
- 5 cups of vegetable broth

COOKING STEPS

1. Heat the oil in a nonstick skillet that is placed over a moderate flame; now, cook the garlic in the hot oil until golden, approximately 3 minutes; reserve the garlic.

2. Simply put the other ingredients into your cooker. Add the toasted garlic and gently stir until everything is well incorporated. Seal the cooker according to the manufacturer's directions.

3. Select "Manual" mode and 9-minute cooking time. Once cooking is complete, release pressure manually. Serve with homemade croutons if desired. Bon appétit!

Vegetables and Side Dishes | Instant Pot Cookbook

12. CRAVE-WORTHY AROMATIC POTATO SOUP

 8 Servings

 Ready in about 25 minutes

PER SERVING:
247 Calories; 8.4g Fat; 38.2g Carbs; 5.9g Protein; 4.7g Sugars

This simple but endlessly crave-worthy soup is both sophisticated and rustic. It contains Mediterranean herbs but you can also try sprinkling in a pinch of paprika or chili powder.

INGREDIENTS

- 1 tablespoon butter
- 1 shallot, chopped
- 2 garlic cloves, minced
- 2 ½ cups vegetable stock
- 8 medium-sized baking potatoes, peeled and cubed
- 1 celery stalk, diced
- 1 teaspoon dried basil
- 1 teaspoon dried oregano
- 1/2 teaspoon dried rosemary
- 2 thyme sprigs, leaves chopped
- Fine sea salt and ground black pepper, to your liking
- 1 cup milk
- 1 (8-ounce) container sour cream
- 1 heaping tablespoon fresh Italian parsley, roughly chopped

COOKING STEPS

1. Choose the "Sauté" button to preheat the Instant Pot. Now, melt the butter and stir in the shallot and garlic; sauté for about 4 minutes or until just tender and fragrant.

2. Next, pour in 3/4 cup of stock and stir to scrape off any brown bits from the bottom of the Instant Pot. Now add the potatoes, celery, and all seasonings; stir to combine well.

3. Cook for 10 minutes at HIGH pressure. Afterward, perform a quick release and open the pot. Then, pour in the remaining stock, milk, and sour cream.

4. Purée with an emersion blender until your desired consistency is reached. Adjust seasonings to taste and serve warm in individual soup bowls garnished with fresh Italian parsley. Bon appétit!

13. HEARTY VEGETABLES WITH WHEAT BERRIES

 6 Servings

 Ready in about 20 minutes

PER SERVING:
101 Calories; 3.9g Fat; 15.6g Carbs; 2.4g Protein; 1.6g Sugars

Pressure cooked wheat berries are chewy and flavorsome. This versatile whole grain goes well with your favorite vegetables. In this recipe, the secret lies in the simple approach – sauté the vegetables to enhance the flavor.

INGREDIENTS

- 1 ½ cups white wheat berries
- 6 cups water
- 1 ½ tablespoons olive oil
- 1 leek, thinly sliced
- 2 green garlic stalks, sliced
- 2 large-sized carrots, chopped
- 2 medium-sized parsnips, chopped
- Salt and ground black peppercorns, to savor
- 1 teaspoon paprika
- 1/4 teaspoon cumin powder
- 1/4 teaspoon turmeric powder
- 1/2 teaspoon fennel seeds
- 1/2 teaspoon celery seeds

COOKING STEPS

1. Place white wheat berries in water and soak overnight.

2. Then, heat olive oil in a skillet; now, cook the leek, green garlic, carrots, and parsnip until tender; it will take 4 to 5 minutes.

3. Then, press the "Multi-grain" button and pressure cook wheat berries with all seasonings. Open the Instant Pot according to the manufacturer's instructions.

4. Finally, stir in the sautéed vegetables and serve with sour cream. Bon appétit!

14. YELLOW WAX BEAN CASSEROLE

 4 Servings

 Ready in about 30 minutes

PER SERVING: 207 Calories; 9.9 Fat; 25.3 Carbs; 7.6g Protein; 9.3g Sugars

The casserole is definitely one of the best options to make your luncheon a delicious pleasure. In this recipe, you can substitute freshly shredded Cheddar for Asiago with the same result.

INGREDIENTS

- 1 ½ tablespoons butter, softened
- 1 purple onion, thinly sliced
- 2 garlic cloves, pressed
- 2 carrots, thinly sliced
- 1 parsnip, thinly sliced
- 1/3 cup cream of onion soup
- 3/4 pound yellow wax beans, trimmed
- 1 red bell pepper, deveined and thinly sliced
- 1 green bell pepper, deveined and thinly sliced
- Salt and freshly ground black pepper, to your liking
- 1 teaspoon cumin powder
- 1/2 teaspoon cayenne pepper
- 1/2 cup Asiago cheese, shaved

COOKING STEPS

1. Preheat your cooker on "Sauté" function. Now, melt the butter and cook the onion until just tender. You can add water, one spoon at a time, to prevent from sticking to the bottom.

2. Next, stir in the garlic, carrots, and parsnips and continue sautéing until they are just fragrant. Press the "Cancel" button and add the cream of onion soup to deglaze your pot.

3. Then, put the beans in; add the peppers, salt, black pepper, cumin powder, and cayenne pepper; gently stir to combine well.

4. Lock the lid into place, adjust the timer, and pressure cook for 1 minute at HIGH pressure. After that, allow pressure to drop by the quick release method and carefully remove the cooker's lid.

5. At this point, you can simmer the ingredients until the liquid has evaporated. Scrape the mixture into a casserole dish.

6. Bake for 15 minutes in the preheated oven; finally, top your casserole with Asiago and bake for 5 minutes longer, or until the casserole is warmed through. Bon appétit!

15. MAPLE AND BALSAMIC SWEET POTATO MASH

 8 Servings

 Ready in about 20 minutes

PER SERVING:
191 Calories; 4.5g Fat; 36.0g Carbs; 2.6g Protein; 12.2g Sugars

Preparing sweet potato mash in the Instant Pot is not only fun, it's also very simple. Sweet potato mash is quite versatile food so let your imagination run wild!

INGREDIENTS

- 2 ½ pounds sweet potatoes, peeled and diced
- 2 spring onions, chopped
- 1/3 teaspoon black pepper
- 1/2 teaspoon fine sea salt
- 1/2 teaspoon minced coriander
- 2 sprigs rosemary, chopped
- 1/2 teaspoon dried basil
- 1 teaspoon oregano
- 3 tablespoons milk
- 2 tablespoons heavy cream
- 1/4 cup of maple syrup
- 1 tablespoon balsamic vinegar
- 2 tablespoons butter

COOKING STEPS

1. Place the trivet into your Instant Pot; add 1 ¼ cups of water to the bottom. Put the sweet potatoes and the spring onions on the trivet and pressure cook them for 8 minutes using HIGH pressure.

2. When pressure cooking is done, allow the pressure to come down using a quick release.

3. Purée sweet potatoes and spring onions until smooth and uniform. Throw the remaining ingredients into the warm potato mash and serve immediately!

CHICKEN RECIPES

16. ZESTY CHICKEN WITH APRICOT SAUCE

 6 Servings

 Ready in about 20 minutes

PER SERVING:
324 Calories; 7.0g Fat; 16.4g Carbs; 44.4 Protein; 12.4g Sugars

The apricot sauce adds a fruity taste to this amazing chicken recipe, making chicken meals less boring and more appealing! One tablespoon of light soy sauce works well with this sauce, too.

INGREDIENTS

- 1 tablespoon olive oil
- 1 small-sized whole chicken, cut into pieces with bones
- 1 onion, cut into wedges
- Sea salt flakes and red pepper flakes, to taste
- 1/2 teaspoon dried marjoram
- 1/4 cup white wine
- 1/4 cup chicken broth
- 1 ½ tablespoons rice wine vinegar

For the Sauce:

- 1/4 cup apricot preserves
- 1 ½ tablespoons rice wine vinegar
- 2 tablespoons honey
- Salt, to taste

COOKING STEPS

1. Put the olive oil, chicken, onion wedges, sea salt flakes, red pepper flakes, marjoram, wine, chicken broth, and rice wine vinegar, into your Instant Pot.

2. Then, cook on HIGH pressure for 10 minutes. When the timer beeps, perform a quick pressure release. Taste for doneness and transfer to a nice serving platter.

3. Add the sauce ingredients to the pot, press "Sauté" key and cook for 8 to 10 minutes or until the sauce has reduced to a syrupy consistency.

4. Pour over the chicken and serve right away. Bon appétit!

17. ORANGE MARMALADE-GLAZED CHICKEN THIGHS

 8 Servings

 Ready in about 20 minutes

PER SERVING:
270 Calories; 10.3g Fat; 9.2g Carbs; 33.6g Protein; 6.6g Sugars

This is an elegant and flavorsome chicken meal for the perfect weeknight dinner. Serve this irresistible combination of saucy chicken thighs and orange over hot rice.

INGREDIENTS

- 1 tablespoon sesame oil
- 1 shallot, peeled and cut into wedges
- 3 cloves garlic, finely minced
- 1 teaspoon fresh grated ginger
- 2 pounds bone-in chicken thighs, skinless
- 1 teaspoon coarse salt
- 3/4 teaspoon chili powder
- 1/2 teaspoon cumin powder
- 10 ounces orange-flavored carbonated beverage
- 2 tablespoons orange marmalade
- 1 ½ tablespoons soy sauce

COOKING STEPS

1. Preheat your Instant Pot by selecting the "Sauté" button; heat the sesame oil.

2. Now, sauté the shallot, garlic, and ginger in the hot oil until just tender and aromatic; make sure to stir frequently.

3. Next step, stir in the chicken thighs, coarse salt, chili powder, and cumin powder; cook for 2 to 3 more minutes.

4. Then, pour in the orange-flavored carbonated beverage to scrape up any browned bits from the bottom of your cooker. After that, stir in the orange marmalade and soy sauce; stir well and lock the lid. Pressure cook for 5 minutes at HIGH pressure.

5. Press "Cancel" and release the pressure naturally. Carefully remove the lid, check for doneness and serve warm.

18. WINTER SPICY CHICKEN SOUP

 4 Servings

 Ready in about 20 minutes

PER SERVING:
121 Calories; 6.1 Fat; 6.5g Carbs; 10.1 Protein; 4.0g Sugars

This light chicken soup is both dinner-worthy and healthy lunch option. You will love this recipe, especially on windy winter days.

INGREDIENTS

- 1 tablespoon peanut oil
- 1 garlic clove, chopped
- 1 medium-sized chicken breast, chopped
- 1 teaspoon shallot powder
- 1/2 teaspoon porcini powder
- 1/2 teaspoon fennel seeds
- Salt, to taste
- 1 (14.5-ounce) can tomatoes, diced
- 2 cups chicken broth
- 1/2 cup mild salsa
- Sour cream, to serve
- 1/4 cup fresh parsley, chopped

COOKING STEPS

1. Firstly, press the "Sauté" key and heat the peanut oil; then, cook the garlic until just browned. Now, add the chicken and stir for a few minutes; add the seasonings, tomatoes, and broth. Bring it to a boil.

2. Pressure cook for 8 to 10 minutes at HIGH pressure. After that, allow pressure to drop on its own; then, carefully open the Instant Pot.

3. Stir in salsa; heat through before serving. Serve in individual bowls dolloped with sour cream and topped with fresh parsley.

19. LOADED CHICKEN SAUSAGE PILAF

 4 Servings

 Ready in about 30 minutes

PER SERVING: 301 Calories; 5.5g Fat; 39.8g Carbs; 20.7g Protein; 1.0 Sugars

This recipe omits the usual chicken meat, replacing it with extra spicy chicken sausage. Also, you can top this casserole with shaved cheese and bake it in the preheated oven. Yummy!

INGREDIENTS

- 1 tablespoon lard
- 1/2 pound chicken sausage, sliced
- 1 shallot, peeled and diced
- 1 celery stalk, chopped
- 1 carrot, chopped
- 1 jalapeño pepper, seeded and minced
- 3/4 cup chicken broth
- 1 ¼ cups lukewarm water
- 1 cup Arborio rice
- 1/4 teaspoon dried marjoram
- 1/2 teaspoon dried thyme
- 1/2 teaspoon cayenne pepper
- Salt and ground black pepper, to your liking

COOKING STEPS

1. Preheat your pot using the "Sauté" setting; melt the lard and cook the sausage along with the shallots, celery, carrot, and minced jalapeño pepper until just tender.

2. Pour in the broth and scrape up any browned bits from the bottom of your pot; use a wooden spoon.

3. In a heat-proof bowl, place the water and rice. Insert a steamer rack into the cooker; place the bowl onto the rack.

4. Cook at HIGH pressure for approximately 4 minutes. Afterwards, allow the cooker to release pressure on its own.

5. Then, combine the chicken sausage mixture with rice mixture and remaining seasonings; bake in the preheated oven for about 5 minutes. Eat warm.

20. GREEN BEAN, SNAP PEA AND CHICKEN SOUP

 6 Servings

 Ready in about 20 minutes

PER SERVING:
159 Calories; 11.3g Fat; 7.9g Carbs; 8.3g Protein; 3.3g Sugars

This soup is not only easy to cook, but it is full of valuable nutrients too. It is loaded with fresh vegetables and looks beautiful on your dining table.

INGREDIENTS

- 4 cups water
- 1 cup non-dairy milk
- 1/2 teaspoon fresh ginger, grated
- 1/2 teaspoon turmeric powder
- 2 carrots, trimmed and chopped
- 1/2 pound green beans
- 1 cup sugar snap peas
- 1 ½ cups chicken breast, cooked and shredded

COOKING STEPS

1. Simply put all of the above ingredients into your Instant Pot. Stir to combine well.

2. Then, choose "Soup" mode. Once cooking is complete, use a quick release; carefully remove the cooker's lid.

3. Serve right away in individual bowls.

21. SAUCY SAGE CHICKEN LEGS

 6 Servings

 Ready in about 20 minutes

PER SERVING:
263 Calories; 13.7g Fat; 1.6g Carbs; 30.7g Protein; 0.0g Sugars

These tender and aromatic chicken legs can be served on any occasion. Don't forget to add a pinch of freshly grated nutmeg for some extra oomph!

INGREDIENTS

- 1 ½ pounds boneless skinless chicken legs, excess fat removed
- 2 garlic cloves, finely chopped
- A pinch of freshly grated nutmeg
- 3/4 cup lime juice
- 1/3 cup tamari sauce
- 2 tablespoons sesame oil
- 1 tablespoon fresh sage, chopped
- 1 tablespoon fresh coriander, chopped
- 1/2 teaspoon coarse salt
- 2 tablespoons dry white wine such as Sauvignon Blanc or Chardonnay

COOKING STEPS

1. Add all of the above ingredients to a resalable bag. Shake to coat well.

2. Place the ingredients into your Instant pot. Press the "Poultry" button and adjust the timer for 12 minutes.

3. Once cooking is done, use a quick release and carefully remove the lid. You can pierce the chicken with a fork to check for doneness.

4. Taste, adjust seasonings and serve warm. Bon appétit!

22. HARVEST CHICKEN STEW WITH SWEET POTATOES

 8 Servings

 Ready in about 25 minutes

PER SERVING:
231 Calories; 9.2 Fat; 8.7g Carbs; 26.1 Protein; 3.4g Sugars

Many homemade cooks like budget-friendly meals in which they can use leftovers. This appetizing chicken stew showcases sweet potato at its finest.

INGREDIENTS

- 1 ½ tablespoons peanut oil
- 1 ½ cups scallions, finely chopped
- 2 garlic cloves, peeled and finely minced
- 1 large-sized parsnip, trimmed and chopped
- 1 large-sized carrot, trimmed and chopped
- 3 ½ cups vegetable stock
- 1/3 cup white wine
- 1 tablespoon light soy sauce
- 4 sweet potatoes, peeled and diced
- 1 ½ pounds leftover chicken meat
- 1 teaspoon smoked cayenne pepper
- 1/2 teaspoon sea salt flakes
- 1/2 teaspoons dried basil
- 1 teaspoon dried rosemary
- 1 (15-ounce) can crushed tomatoes with juice
- 1 cup collard greens, torn into pieces

COOKING STEPS

1. Preheat your cooker by selecting the "Sauté" mode. After that, heat the peanut oil; now, sauté the scallions, garlic, parsnip, and carrots for about 4 minutes or until just tender and fragrant.

2. Add the other ingredients and stir to combine well. Cover with the lid and press the "Soup" button.

3. Cook for 10 minutes at HIGH pressure. Once pressure cooking is complete, use a quick release. Open the cooker and serve. Bon appétit!

23. Easy Chicken Basmati Risotto

 8 Servings

 Ready in about 30 minutes

PER SERVING:
239 Calories; 5.4 Fat; 26.3g Carbs; 19.5g Protein; 0.7g Sugars

This recipe is very easy but it has a rich taste thanks to the carefully selected seasonings. If you could use a roasted vegetable broth, it will be even better!

INGREDIENTS

- 1 cup basmati rice
- 1 cup water
- 4 cups vegetable broth
- 2 cloves garlic, minced
- 1 tablespoon olive oil
- 1/2 teaspoon kosher salt
- 1/4 teaspoon red pepper flakes, crushed
- 1 sweet paprika
- 1/2 teaspoon dried dill weed
- 1 tablespoon dry mustard
- 1/3 teaspoon bay leaf powder
- 2 cups chicken leftover, chopped

COOKING STEPS

1. Add all ingredients, minus the leftover chicken, to your Instant Pot; stir to combine well.

2. Lock the lid into place and choose the "Rice" setting. Release the pressure naturally.

3. Uncover your cooker, add the chicken and simmer over a moderate heat until the liquid has evaporated. Serve immediately.

24. CREAMY FETTUCCINE WITH CHICKEN AND MUSHROOMS

 6 Servings

 Ready in about 25 minutes

PER SERVING:
411 Calories; 18.8 Fat; 35.2g Carbs; 24.7g Protein; 1.5g Sugars

This is a great comfort food with a little spicy kick! If you don't have a lemon thyme, substitute with regular thyme and a pinch of grated ginger.

INGREDIENTS

- 1 ½ tablespoons olive oil
- 2 cups frozen chicken, cubed
- 1 teaspoon lemon thyme
- 1 cup mushrooms
- 3/4 pound egg fettuccine pasta
- 2 cups cream of mushroom soup
- 1 cup water
- 2 tablespoons butter, at room temperature
- 3/4 cup cream
- 3/4 cup Cheddar cheese, shredded
- Sea salt and ground black pepper, to taste

COOKING STEPS

1. Place the first 7 ingredients in your Instant Pot. Lock the lid into place and choose "Manual" setting. Pressure cook for 10 minutes.

2. Meanwhile, make the sauce. Heat the pan over a moderate flame and warm the butter; stir in the cream and turn the heat to low; let it simmer for 4 to 6 minutes.

3. Now, fold in the cheese and whisk, heating through. When pressure cooking is completed, add the sauce to the chicken mixture; season with salt and pepper to taste.

4. Lastly, gently stir to combine and serve in individual soup bowls garnished with fresh chives. Bon appétit!

25. SUPER CHEESY CHICKEN PARMESAN

 6 Servings

 Ready in about 20 minutes

PER SERVING:
286 Calories; 8.3g Fat; 23.2g Carbs; 31.6g Protein; 8.6 Sugars

With fresh scallions, earthy-flavored chipotle peppers, and mellow Parmesan, this recipe is flavorful and extremely comforting. Parmigiano-Reggiano or Parmesan cheese in one of the best flavor-enhancing ingredients you can ever use!

INGREDIENTS

- 1 tablespoon butter
- 2 chicken breasts, boneless, skinless and chopped
- 1 cup scallions, finely minced
- 2-3 cloves garlic, finely minced
- 1 red bell pepper, deveined and chopped
- 1 chipotle pepper, deveined and chopped
- 1 ¼ cups tomato paste
- 1/2 cup all-purpose flour
- 1/4 teaspoon red pepper flakes, crushed
- 1 teaspoon garlic salt
- Freshly cracked mixed peppercorns, to taste
- 1/2 teaspoon sweet paprika
- 1 ½ teaspoons stock powder, preferably homemade
- 3/4 cup Parmesan cheese, freshly grated
- 1 heaping tablespoon fresh parsley

COOKING STEPS

1. Press the "Sauté" button to preheat your Instant Pot. Now, brown the chicken on all sides; stir in the scallions, garlic, and both peppers. Cook for a further few minutes or until the scallions are just tender and the peppers are aromatic.

2. After that, add the remaining ingredients, minus the cheese and parsley; stir until everything is well incorporated and seal the cooker.

3. Now, choose "Manual" option; pressure cook for 11 minutes. Then, turn the valve to allow the steam to escape.

4. Carefully and slowly remove the lid; fold in freshly grated Parmesan cheese. Serve sprinkled with fresh parsley. Bon appétit!

26. MEXICAN-STYLE CHICKEN CHILI

 10 Servings

 Ready in about 20 minutes

PER SERVING:
442 Calories; 5.3g Fat; 59.6g Carbs; 36.0g Protein; 5.4g Sugars

Here's an easy and quick way to cook a satisfying chili for you family. Fresh basil and cilantro provide a depth of herbal flavor, while vodka and horseradish complete the meal with their sharp and extraordinary notes.

INGREDIENTS

- 1 ½ tablespoons olive oil
- 3/4 cup red onions, chopped
- 1 ¼ pounds chicken, ground
- 1 teaspoon minced fresh garlic
- 2 green peppers, deveined and diced
- 1 teaspoon ground cumin
- 1 teaspoon freshly grated horseradish
- 5 ½ cups canned tomatoes, diced
- 2 ounces vodka
- 1 tablespoon chili powder
- 2 (15-ounce) cans pinto beans, drained and rinsed
- Several dashes of Worcestershire sauce
- 1 cup water
- 1/2 teaspoon fresh lemon juice
- 1 tablespoon basil leaves, roughly chopped
- Several dashes of Tabasco
- 1 tablespoon fresh cilantro, roughly chopped

COOKING STEPS

1. Press the "Sauté" key to preheat your Instant Pot. Now, warm the olive oil; sauté red onions until translucent.

2. Stir in the ground chicken and cook until it is browned; stir in minced garlic and peppers and cook for just 1 more minute.

3. After that, add the ground cumin, horseradish, canned tomatoes, vodka, chili powder, and beans; stir, bringing to a boil.

4. Next step, add Worcestershire sauce, water, lemon and basil. Now, fasten the lid on the Instant Pot; pressure cook for 6 minutes at HIGH pressure.

5. When the time is over, perform a quick pressure release. Divide among soup bowls and add Tabasco and fresh cilantro. Serve with tortilla chips, guacamole or sour cream if desired.

27. AUTUMN CHICKEN AND CAULIFLOWER SOUP

 4 Servings

 Ready in about 35 minutes

PER SERVING:
191 Calories; 3.3g Fat; 13.4g Carbs; 26.7g Protein; 5.3g Sugars

A medley of fine chicken meat and vegetables are flavored with amazing spices in this super-healthy soup. If you are not in a hurry, sweat or brown the onion before pressure cooking.

INGREDIENTS

- 3/4 pound frozen chicken, boneless and skinless
- 1 small yellow onion, peeled and sliced
- 2 carrots, trimmed and chopped
- 1 cup cauliflower florets
- 1 parsnip, trimmed and chopped
- 3 ½ cups chicken stock
- 1/2 teaspoon kosher salt
- 1/4 teaspoon ground black peppercorns
- 1/2 teaspoon bay leaf powder
- A pinch of grated nutmeg

COOKING STEPS

1. Simply place all of the above ingredients into your electric pressure cooker.

2. Press the "Manual" button. Fasten the lid on the cooker and pressure cook for 32 minutes.

3. Next, turn off the cooker and open the lid once the pressure is completely released.

4. Serve with enough crusty bread. Bon appétit!

28. ROMANO MEATBALLS IN CHEESY SAUCE

 4 Servings

 Ready in about 45 minutes

PER SERVING:
329 Calories; 18.0g Fat; 9.0g Carbs; 31.4g Protein; 0.0g Sugars

Say cheese and enjoy these saucy chicken meatballs! Alternatively, you can use some chili powder to add extra warmth to this appetizing dish.

INGREDIENTS

- 3/4 pound ground chicken
- 1/2 cup crushed saltines
- 1/3 cup Romano cheese, freshly grated
- 2 garlic cloves, finely minced
- 1/4 cup scallions, finely chopped
- 2 tablespoons cilantro, chopped
- Sea salt and ground black pepper, to your liking
- 1 egg, beaten
- 1 ½ cups vegetable stock
- 1 ½ tablespoons olive oil
- 1 ½ tablespoons cornstarch
- 3 tablespoons water
- 1/4 cup crème fraiche
- 1/3 cup Ricotta cheese

COOKING STEPS

1. Mix the first eight ingredients; shape into bite-sized balls. Place in the refrigerator for 30 to 40 minutes.

2. Pour in the vegetable stock and stir to combine. Lightly grease a steamer rack using a cooking spray. Now, insert the steamer rack into the cooker; lay the meatballs on the steamer rack.

3. Seal the lid and pressure cook at HIGH pressure for 5 minutes. Afterwards, release the pressure naturally. Take away the lid.

4. Heat olive oil in a nonstick skillet over a moderate heat; brown the meatballs on all sides. To make a slurry, dissolve cornstarch in water.

5. Click the "Sauté" button and bring the vegetable stock to a boil. Whisk in crème fraiche; add the slurry and cook until the sauce has thickened. Stir in Ricotta cheese.

6. Throw the meatballs into the sauce. Bon appétit!

29. Hot Paprika Wings with Sesame Green Beans

 8 Servings

 Ready in about 25 minutes

PER SERVING:
347 Calories; 12.8g Fat; 4.9g Carbs; 50.5g Protein; 1.1g Sugars

Seasoned with paprika and soaked in hot sauce, these wings have a unique flavor that brings a twist to your everyday dinner. The wings go perfectly with green beans.

INGREDIENTS

- 3 pounds chicken wings
- 1 teaspoon paprika
- 1 teaspoon cumin powder
- 1 teaspoon granulated garlic
- 1/2 teaspoon onion powder
- Salt and ground black pepper, to taste
- 1/3 cup balsamic vinegar
- 1/4 cup hot sauce
- 2 tablespoons Worchester sauce
- 1 pound green beans
- Salt and pepper, to taste
- 1 tablespoon toasted sesame seeds, for garnish

COOKING STEPS

1. Add the chicken wings, seasonings, vinegar, hot sauce, and Worchester sauce to your Instant Pot electric pressure cooker.

2. Choose "Poultry" function, seal the cooker, and pressure cook for 15 minutes. Transfer to a serving bowl.

3. After that, clean your pot and throw in the green beans; season with salt and pepper to taste. Pressure cook for 5 minutes; sprinkle with toasted sesame seeds and serve with prepared chicken wings. Bon appétit!

30. ASIAN-STYLE CURRY AND TOMATO CHICKEN

 8 Servings

 Ready in about 30 minutes

PER SERVING:
344 Calories; 19.6g Fat; 6.7g Carbs; 34.5g Protein; 2.3g Sugars

Flavorful chicken bites in the creamed spicy sauce! You'll be able to enhance the flavor of this meal by including Habanero pepper as an alternative to usual chili powder. Enjoy!

INGREDIENTS

- 2 tablespoons olive oil
- 3 chicken breasts, chopped into bite-sized chunks
- 1 Habanero pepper, deveined and chopped
- 2 ½ cups tomato pure
- 1 tablespoon ketchup
- 1 teaspoon sea salt flakes
- 1 teaspoon porcini powder
- 3/4 teaspoon celery seeds
- 1/2 teaspoon mustard powder
- 3/4 tablespoon smoked cayenne pepper
- 1/2 cup heavy cream
- 3/4 cup sour cream
- 1 teaspoon black cardamom
- 1 Indian bay leaf
- 1 tablespoon curry powder
- 1/4 teaspoon rubbed sage
- 2 tablespoons cornstarch
- 2 tablespoons water

COOKING STEPS

1. Select the "Sauté" function and warm the olive oil. Then, brown the chicken chunks on all sides for about 3 minutes. Reserve.

2. Add Habanero pepper and cook for 15 seconds, stirring frequently. Add the remaining ingredients, minus the cornstarch and water.

3. Place the lid and cook for 4 minutes at HIGH pressure. Lastly, release the pressure naturally. Place the chicken on a serving platter.

4. Make a slurry by whisking the cornstarch and water. Stir into the pot and push the "Sauté" key. Bring to a boil and press the "Cancel" key. Eat warm.

TURKEY RECIPES

31. OLD-FASHIONED TURKEY WITH KIDNEY BEANS

 6 Servings

 Ready in about 45 minutes

PER SERVING:
275 Calories; 7.5g Fat; 22.9g Carbs; 28.4g Protein; 2.4g Sugars

When time is up, check your beans for doneness. If your beans aren't soft enough, return to high pressure for 2 to 3 minutes more. This recipe has a delightful taste thanks to the aromatic Mediterranean herbs.

INGREDIENTS

- 1 ½ tablespoons vegetable oil
- 1 leek, chopped
- 1 garlic clove, chopped
- 1 sweet pepper, deveined and chopped
- 3/4 pound turkey, ground
- 1/2 cup turkey ham, chopped
- Salt and freshly ground black pepper, to taste
- 1 teaspoon dried thyme
- 1 teaspoon coriander
- 1 teaspoon bay leaf powder
- 1 cup canned kidney beans
- 1 cup of water
- 1 ¼ cups of bone broth

COOKING STEPS

1. Press the "Sauté" button and heat the oil; then, sauté the leeks, garlic, sweet peppers. Cook for approximately 4 minutes or until the vegetables are aromatic.

2. After that, stir in the turkey, turkey ham, salt, black pepper, thyme, coriander, and bay leaf powder; cook about 9 minutes.

3. Next, throw in the beans, water, and bone broth. Secure the lid, choose "Bean/Chili" setting, and adjust the timer for 28 minutes.

4. Once cooking is complete, push the "Cancel" button; finally, perform a natural release. Bon appétit!

32. MUSTARD TURKEY BREASTS WITH HERB GRAVY

 6 Servings

 Ready in about 40 minutes

PER SERVING:
207 Calories; 2.9g Fat;
14.3 Carbs; 29.8g Protein;
6.7g Sugars

For the very first time, make the recipe as written; later, you can experiment with herbs according to your taste. Serve the turkey breasts with your favorite sides such as pickled or fresh salad.

INGREDIENTS

- 4 pounds turkey breasts
- 1 ½ tablespoons whole-grain mustard
- 1 fine sea salt
- 1/2 teaspoon freshly ground black pepper, or more to taste
- 1/3 teaspoon cayenne pepper
- 1 cup of vegetable stock
- 1 cup shallots, cut into wedges
- 2 garlic cloves, peeled and pressed
- 2 carrots, sliced
- 1/2 teaspoon dried basil
- 2 tablespoons cornstarch
- 2 tablespoons water
- 1 teaspoon dried rosemary
- 2 fresh sage sprigs
- 1 ½ heaping tablespoons fresh Italian parsley, chopped

COOKING STEPS

1. Rub the turkey breast with mustard; then season them with salt, black pepper, and cayenne pepper.

2. After that, choose "Sauté" setting and sear turkey breast on all sides. Pour in the vegetable stock and deglaze the bottom. Now, stir in the shallots, garlic, carrots, and basil.

3. Put on the lid of your cooker and seal; pressure cook for 30 minutes at HIGH pressure.

4. When the cycle is complete, allow the pressure to come down naturally. When the meat has reached 165 degrees F, it's done. Transfer the meat to a serving platter.

5. In a small bowl, mix the cornstarch and water to make the slurry. Add the slurry to the pot along with the rosemary and the sage.

6. Press the "Sauté" key and stir until cooking liquid has thickened. Serve garnished with Italian parsley. Bon appétit!

33. TURKEY SAUSAGE WITH CREAMY BROCCOLI

 6 Servings

 Ready in about 15 minutes

PER SERVING:
257 Calories; 12.4g Fat; 18.0g Carbs; 22.3g Protein; 5.0g Sugars

This is a delicious one-pot meal and it takes just a few minutes to be placed into the cooker. This recipe cooks the broccoli florets until they are soft only in the middle, but they aren't overcooked and mushy. Enjoy!

INGREDIENTS

- 1 medium-sized head broccoli, broken into florets
- 1 large-sized yellow onion, peeled and cut into wedges
- 1 teaspoon coarse salt
- 1/2 teaspoon ground mixed peppercorns
- 1/2 teaspoon smoked cayenne pepper
- 1/2 teaspoon dried dill weed
- 1/3 cup heavy cream
- 1 ½ tablespoons olive oil
- 1 ½ cups turkey sausage, sliced

COOKING STEPS

1. Prepare your Instant Pot by adding 1 cup of water and a trivet. Place a steamer basket on top of the trivet. Place the broccoli and onion in the steamer basket.

2. Close the lid, choose "Manual" and pressure cook for 5 minutes at HIGH pressure. Finally, perform a quick pressure release and carefully remove the lid.

3. Rinse the vegetables and transfer them into a nice serving bowl; add the salt, peppercorns, cayenne pepper, dill, and heavy cream; gently stir to combine.

4. Preheat olive oil on "Sauté" function. Cook the sausage until no longer pink. Serve with broccoli side dish. Bon appétit!

34. CURRIED TURKEY AND OKRA SOUP

 6 Servings

 Ready in about 40 minutes

PER SERVING:
140 Calories; 10.3g Fat; 6.9g Carbs; 6.5g Protein; 3.6g Sugars

This richly flavored leftover turkey soup is a perfect second-day dish after Thanksgiving. Comforting, warming and economical! Okra is also known as ladies' fingers, bhindi or gumbo. This flowering plant is a nutritional powerhouse so it has many health benefits.

INGREDIENTS

- 2 cups of water
- 1 cup of bone broth
- 1 can almond milk
- 1 teaspoon curry powder
- 1 teaspoon ground ginger
- 1/2 teaspoon paprika
- 2 medium-sized carrots, timed and thinly sliced
- 3/4 cup okra, frozen
- 1 cup leftover turkey breast, chopped
- Salt and black pepper, to your liking

COOKING STEPS

1. Simply place all the ingredients into your Instant Pot. Gently stir until everything is well incorporated. Secure the lid.

2. Now, choose "Soup" setting. Once the cooking is complete, use a natural release for about 25 minutes. Remove the lid according to the manual.

3. Taste and adjust the seasonings. Divide among individual bowls and serve right away.

35. THANKSGIVING CLASSIC TURKEY WITH GRAVY

 4 Servings

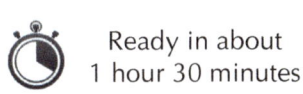 Ready in about 1 hour 30 minutes

PER SERVING:
231 Calories; 6.1g Fat;
5.6g Carbs; 36.1g Protein;
0.0g Sugars

Don't want to cook a whole bird for Thanksgiving? Here's a great alternative and delicious festive classic dish. Add mashed potatoes if desired and delight your family!

INGREDIENTS

- 3/4 pound turkey breast, diced
- 1 cup turkey or chicken stock
- 1 ½ tablespoons balsamic vinegar
- 1/4 teaspoon turmeric
- 3/4 cup scallions, chopped
- 1 clove garlic, minced
- 2 sprigs rosemary, crushed
- 1 sprig thyme, crushed
- 1/2 teaspoon kosher salt
- 1/4 teaspoon ground black pepper

For the Gravy:

- 2 ½ tablespoons all-purpose flour
- 1/4 cup of water

COOKING STEPS

1. Click "Sauté" button to preheat your pot; now, cook the turkey until just browned.

2. Then, add the stock, vinegar, turmeric, scallions, garlic, rosemary, thyme, salt, and black pepper. Stir, secure the lid, and choose "Poultry" mode. Pressure cook for about 1 hour 10 minutes.

3. Perform a quick pressure release and reserve the turkey.

4. To make the gravy, whisk flour and water until well incorporated. Add the mixture to the pot.

5. Then, set the cooker to "Keep Warm" function and let it cook for 12 to 16 minutes or until the gravy has thickened. Serve with reserved meat.

36. COUNTRY-STYLE GROUND TURKEY STEW WITH NOODLES

 8 Servings

 Ready in about 40 minutes

PER SERVING:
143 Calories; 5.4g Fat; 16.4g Carbs; 8.3g Protein; 3.6g Sugars

You can make this rich and satisfying soup at the end of the summer, when we have plenty of fresh ripe tomatoes. Egg noodles, any type of them, are a must in this recipe.

INGREDIENTS

- 1 ½ tablespoons butter, at room temperature
- 1/3 pound ground turkey
- Salt and black pepper, to your liking
- 1 cup shallots, diced
- 1 large-sized carrot, trimmed and chopped
- 1 parsnip, cleaned and chopped
- 1 sweet bell pepper, deveined and chopped
- 1 Habanero chili pepper, deveined and chopped
- 1/2 teaspoon marjoram
- 1/2 teaspoon dried rosemary
- 1 teaspoon granulated garlic
- 1/2 teaspoon dried thyme
- 2 tablespoons red wine
- 2 medium-sized tomatoes, seeded and chopped
- 6 cups vegetable stock
- 1 tablespoon fish sauce
- 1/2 teaspoon cayenne pepper
- 8 ounces egg noodles, cooked

COOKING STEPS

1. Choose the "Sauté" function to preheat your Instant Pot. Warm the butter and cook the ground turkey, stirring frequently, until it has browned.

2. Add the salt, pepper, shallots, carrots, parsnip and peppers; cook for a few more minutes or until the vegetables are soft. Add marjoram, rosemary, garlic and thyme; cook until aromatic.

3. Next, add red wine to deglaze the bottom of your pot using a wooden spoon.

4. Then, put the other ingredients in, without the egg noodles. Secure the lid and turn the pot to "Soup" mode; pressure cook for 30 minutes.

5. Finally, perform a quick release; release any remaining steam and open the cooker. Stir in the noodles and serve right away. Bon appétit!

37. SMOKED BARBECUE TURKEY MEATLOAF

 6 Servings

 Ready in about 30 minutes

PER SERVING:
316 Calories; 10.5g Fat; 16.8g Carbs; 37.7g Protein; 9.0g Sugars

Add some nutrition to your festive meatloaf while still achieving amazing results! With less fat and a certain amount of vegetables, this sophisticated dish is sure to please everyone!

INGREDIENTS

- 1 ½ tablespoons butter
- 1 cup scallions, chopped
- 2 garlic cloves, minced
- 1 small celery, chopped
- 1 teaspoon brown sugar
- 14 ounces canned tomato puree
- 2 tablespoons tomato ketchup
- 1/2 teaspoon sea salt flakes
- 1/4 ground black pepper
- 1/4 teaspoon green peppercorns, crushed
- 1 teaspoon smoked cayenne pepper
- 1 cup of loaf bread cubes, toasted
- 1 ½ pounds turkey, ground
- 2 medium-sized eggs
- 1/4 cup of barbecue sauce
- 1 teaspoon Dijon mustard
- A few dashes of liquid smoke
- 3 tablespoons Greek-style yogurt
- 1 tablespoon fish sauce

COOKING STEPS

1. Preheat your Instant Pot on "Sauté" mode; then, melt the butter and sauté the scallions, garlic and celery until tender and fragrant, about 3 minutes.

2. Add brown sugar, tomato puree, ketchup, salt, black pepper, and crushed green peppercorns. Cook until the liquid has almost evaporated. Reserve.

3. Add the rest of the above ingredients to a large mixing dish and mix to combine well. Shape into the loaf and place in a heatproof dish.

4. Pour the tomato sauce over the top of your meatloaf. Cover with foil and pour 2 cups of water to the base of your pot. Insert the trivet and lower the ovenproof dish onto it. Pressure cook using "Meat/Stew" function.

5. Once cooking is complete, push the "Cancel' button and allow the pressure to drop on its own. Serve warm with pressure cooked sweet potato mash. Bon appétit!

38. ONE-POT SPAGHETTI AND TURKEY MEATBALLS

 6 Servings

 Ready in about 25 minutes

PER SERVING: 332 Calories; 11.3g Fat; 37.7g Carbs; 23.8g Protein; 6.9g Sugars

The spaghetti, meatballs, and tomato sauce in your electric pressure cooker! This recipe will provide your family with a great satisfying dish. Don't forget to briefly brown your meatballs to enhance the flavors.

INGREDIENTS

- 3 teaspoons butter
- 2-3 garlic cloves, finely minced
- 1/3 cup scallions, finely chopped
- 1/2 pound butternut squash, peeled and diced
- 2 bell peppers, deveined and chopped
- 2 (14.5-ounce) cans diced tomatoes with juice
- 3/4 pound ground turkey
- 1/4 cup plain breadcrumbs, or more as needed
- 1/4 cup Parmesan cheese
- Fine sea salt and ground black pepper, to taste
- 1 heaping tablespoon fresh mint leaves, finely chopped
- 1 teaspoon marjoram, dried
- 1 teaspoon rosemary, dried
- 8 ounces uncooked spaghetti

COOKING STEPS

1. Choose the "Sauté" setting in order to preheat your cooker. Now, melt the butter and sauté the garlic and scallions until just tender. After that, stir in the squash and bell pepper and continue sautéing for an additional 4 minutes.

2. Add the diced tomatoes with juice and bring to a gentle simmer.

3. Meanwhile, create the meatball mixture by mixing the remaining ingredients, without the spaghetti; mix well to combine. Shape into bite-sized meatballs.

4. Brown your meatballs in a non-stick skillet on all sides. Carefully throw them into the simmering sauce.

5. Select "Manual" setting and cook at HIGH pressure for 8 minutes. Once cooking is complete, press the "Cancel" button and use the quick release. Check the pasta for doneness and serve warm.

39. TURKEY DRUMSTICKS WITH VERMOUTH PAN SAUCE

 6 Servings

 Ready in about 25 minutes

PER SERVING:
312 Calories; 11.8g Fat; 7.1g Carbs; 41.1g Protein; 1.3g Sugars

In this recipe, turkey legs are seared to create a crispy skin and vegetables are sautéed to enhance the flavor. You will use dry vermouth to deglaze the pan as well as to make a royal sauce in your own kitchen. Lovely!

INGREDIENTS

- 2 tablespoons of canola oil
- 2 medium-sized turkey drumsticks
- Garlic salt, to taste
- 1 cup shallots, peeled and chopped
- 1 large-sized carrot, trimmed and chopped
- 1 bell pepper, deveined and chopped
- 2 cloves garlic, minced
- 1 teaspoon marjoram
- 1 teaspoon tarragon
- 1/2 cup dry vermouth
- 1 ¼ cups vegetable broth
- 1 tablespoon Worcester sauce
- 1 teaspoon bay leaf powder
- 1/2 teaspoon ground black pepper
- 1/2 teaspoon cayenne pepper, or more to taste

COOKING STEPS

1. Preheat your Instant Pot on "Sauté" mode. Then, warm 1 tablespoon of canola. Season the turkey drumsticks with enough garlic salt. Now, sear the turkey drumsticks for about 3 minutes; flip them and cook on the other side for further 3 minutes. Reserve.

2. After that, preheat the pot on "Sauté" setting again and heat the remaining 1 tablespoon of canola oil. Now, cook the shallots, carrots, peppers, and garlic until just tender and fragrant. Add marjoram and tarragon; stir for 30 seconds more.

3. Pour in the dry vermouth and stir with a wooden spoon, scraping any brown bits off the bottom of the cooker.

4. Add the rest of the above ingredients. Press "Manual" button and set the cooker to cook at HIGH pressure for 15 minutes.

5. Lastly, allow the pressure to come down naturally; carefully open the lid according to the manual. Serve and enjoy!

40. NANA'S FAMOUS TURKEY CORN CHILI

 8 Servings

 Ready in about 20 minutes

PER SERVING:
366 Calories; 6.9g Fat; 46.3g Carbs; 33.0g Protein; 6.0g Sugars

Make this all-star chili using only one revolutionary kitchen gadget – Instant Pot! This crowd-pleasing chili is quick enough to cook on a weeknight.

INGREDIENTS

- 1 tablespoon lard
- 1 clove garlic, minced
- 1 large-sized shallot, peeled and diced
- 1 Serrano pepper, deveined and chopped
- 1 sweet pepper, deveined and chopped
- 3/4 teaspoon mustard powder
- 1 teaspoon dried basil, crushed
- 1/2 teaspoon hot paprika
- 1 ¼ pounds turkey, chopped
- 1/4 cup water
- 1 bouillon cube
- 10 ounces can red kidney beans, rinsed and mashed
- 14 ounces canned tomatoes with juice
- 5 ounces sweet corn kernels
- 1 teaspoon Tabasco
- 2 bay leaves

COOKING STEPS

1. Preheat your Instant Pot on "Sauté" mode and warm the lard. Then, sauté the garlic, shallots, and peppers until just tender, about 6 minutes.

2. Now, stir in mustard powder, basil and hot paprika and cook for 1 more minute or until fragrant and lightly browned.

3. Place the turkey in and cook, stirring often, for 5 to 6 minutes or until the meat is no longer pink. Crumble the turkey with a fork and add the other ingredients. Secure the lid and turn the cooker to "Bean/Chili" mode.

4. After that, use a natural release method; then, release any remaining steam and remove the lid.

5. Serve in individual bowls, with a dollop of sour cream. Bon appétit!

41. HOLIDAY BALSAMIC TURKEY DRUMETTES

 4 Servings

 Ready in about 45 minutes

PER SERVING:
212 Calories; 5.8g Fat; 3.6g Carbs; 33.8g Protein; 0.0g Sugars

Meaty turkey drumettes cook perfectly in the Instant Pot; further, we will turn cooking juices into a delicious sauce and ladle it over the entire plate. Lovely!

INGREDIENTS

- 1 ½ pounds turkey drumettes
- 1 cup of turkey stock
- 2 ½ tablespoons balsamic vinegar
- 2 cloves garlic, minced
- 1/2 teaspoon dried rosemary
- 1/2 teaspoon dried sage
- Sea salt and ground black pepper, to your liking
- 3 tablespoons flour
- 1/4 cup of water

COOKING STEPS

1. Set the cooker to "Sauté"; spritz the bottom of your Instant Pot with a cooking spray and brown the turkey drumettes. Add the stock and balsamic vinegar and stir with a wooden spatula.

2. Choose the "Poultry" setting and cook for 30 minutes. Allow the pressure to come down naturally and carefully remove the lid. Reserve the prepared turkey drumettes.

3. To make the sauce, whisk the garlic, rosemary, sage, salt, black pepper, flour and water. Add the flour mixture to the cooking liquid in the Instant pot.

4. Turn your Instant Pot to "Keep/Warm" mode and simmer the sauce for 15 minutes. Serve warm over the turkey drumettes.

42. TURKEY CHORIZO AND SPINACH SOUP

 6 Servings

 Ready in about 35 minutes

PER SERVING:
219 Calories; 12.8g Fat; 5.3g Carbs; 20.5g Protein; 2.6g Sugars

The Instant Pot transforms the sausage and regular vegetables into a magical satisfying soup in record time. If you can't find chorizo, use whatever turkey sausage you've got on hand!

INGREDIENTS

- 2 tablespoons canola oil
- 10 ounces cooked turkey chorizo, sliced
- 1 onion, chopped
- 2 garlic cloves, minced
- 1 cup carrots, trimmed and chopped
- 1 cup celery stalks, chopped
- 4 cups of turkey broth
- 3/4 teaspoon salt
- 1/2 freshly ground black pepper
- 1 teaspoon tarragon
- 1 cup spinach, torn into pieces
- 1 tablespoon fresh cilantro, chopped
- 1 cup Monterey Jack cheese, freshly grated

COOKING STEPS

1. Preheat your Instant Pot using "Sauté" mode; now, heat the oil and cook chorizo, onion, garlic, carrot and celery until tender.

2. Stir in the broth, salt, pepper, and tarragon. Then, press the "Soup" button; set the timer for 20 minutes. Then, use a quick release method to release the steam and open the cooker. After that, mash about 1/2 of the mixture and return to the pot.

3. Add the spinach and cook on "Sauté" mode until it is completely wilted and heated through. Serve topped with fresh cilantro and Monterey Jack cheese. Bon appétit!

43. TURKEY CHOWDER WITH SWEET PEAS

 4 Servings

 Ready in about 30 minutes

PER SERVING:
286 Calories; 8.6 Fat; 25.1g Carbs; 25.8g Protein; 11.8g Sugars

You can thicken this chowder with crushed cracker if desired. Sweet peas is added later to keep it from turning mushy. Enjoy!

INGREDIENTS

- 4 slices of turkey bacon, chopped
- 1 turkey wing, boneless
- 1 yellow onion, finely chopped
- 1 teaspoon dried dill weed
- 1 teaspoon granulated garlic
- 1 teaspoon porcini powder
- 1 bay leaf
- 4 cups of bone broth
- 1 medium-sized carrot, chopped
- 2 russet potatoes, peeled and diced
- 1 small-sized bunch parsley, roughly chopped
- 1 can of sweet peas
- 1 cup evaporated milk

COOKING STEPS

1. Preheat your cooker on "Sauté" mode. Then, sear the bacon and turkey wing; add the onions and cook until translucent.

2. Now, add the dill weed, garlic, porcini powder, and bay leaf; cook for just one more minute. Add the rest of the above ingredients, without the peas and the milk. Click "Soup" button and cook for 10 minutes at HIGH pressure.

3. When the cooking is done, use the natural release for 10 minutes, and then, release any remaining steam. Add the sweet peas, milk and simmer on "Keep Warm" function until heated through.

4. Serve at once with oyster crackers if desired. Bon appétit!

44. Easiest Turkey Breast Tenderloin Ever

 4 Servings

 Ready in about 35 minutes

PER SERVING:
219 Calories; 8.6g Fat; 3.7g Carbs; 30.7g Protein; 1.3g Sugars

Here's a great idea for a summer gathering! This is an easy and appetizing family-friendly recipe! If you are not in a hurry, try to marinate this turkey tenderloin with fresh ginger, garlic, and light soy sauce.

INGREDIENTS

- 1 turkey breast tenderloin
- 1 tablespoon olive oil
- 2 cups turkey broth
- 1 cup leek, sliced
- Fine sea salt and pepper, to taste
- 1 bay leaf
- 1 teaspoon dried marjoram

COOKING STEPS

1. Push the "Sauté" button to preheat your Instant Pot. Now, sear the turkey breast in hot olive oil for 2 to 3 minutes on each side.

2. Simply put the remaining ingredients into your Instant Pot. Put the cooker's lid on; make sure the vent is to Sealed.

3. Then, choose "Poultry" mode and cook for 30 minutes at HIGH pressure; perform a natural pressure release.

4. Spoon the cooking liquids over the warm turkey breast tenderloin and serve immediately.

45. SINFULLY DELICIOUS TURKEY RISOTTO

 6 Servings

 Ready in about 25 minutes

PER SERVING:
314 Calories; 7.1g Fat; 47.3g Carbs; 14.0g Protein; 3.7g Sugars

If you like to simplify things, this recipe will be your next favorite. For a more family-friendly recipe, leave out the vermouth and add an extra cup of tomato juice instead.

INGREDIENTS

- 2 tablespoons of olive oil
- 1 small-sized leek, chopped
- 1 turnip, chopped
- 2 carrots, chopped
- 1 teaspoon bay leaf powder
- 1 tablespoon fresh sage leaves, chopped
- 2 cups long grain rice, rinsed
- 3 ½ cups of turkey or roasted vegetable broth
- 1 cup of vermouth
- 1 cup leftover turkey, boneless and chopped
- 1 tablespoon oyster sauce
- Sea salt flakes and freshly cracked black peppercorns, to taste

COOKING STEPS

1. Heat up your cooker on "Sauté" mode; heat the olive oil and sweat the leeks, turnip, and carrots for about 4 minutes; now, add the bay leaf powder and chopped sage leaves and stir for 1 minute more or until aromatic.

2. Add the rest of the above ingredients and seal the lid. Then, choose "Manual" setting and 12-minute cooking time; cook at HIGH pressure.

3. When the cooking is done, use a natural release; make sure to release any remaining steam. Check for doneness and adjust the seasonings as needed.

4. Eat warm with your favorite fresh or pickled salad. Bon appétit!

PORK RECIPES

46

49

53

56

59

46. PERFECT MOIST AND TENDER PULLED PORK

 6 Servings

 Ready in about 55 minutes

PER SERVING:
329 Calories; 12.8g Fat; 2.9g Carbs; 47.9g Protein; 1.4g Sugars

There are so many ways to cook the pork butt, but the secret is to go nicely and slowly. Give this recipe a try and you will see that pressure cooking is one of the best ways to prepare tender pulled pork with little effort.

INGREDIENTS

- 2 pounds pork butt
- 1 teaspoon sea salt flakes
- 1 tablespoon olive oil
- 1/2 teaspoon mixed peppercorns
- 4 cloves garlic, minced
- 1/2 teaspoon basil, fresh or dried
- 1 teaspoon marjoram
- 1 ½ teaspoons mustard seeds
- 1 bay leaf
- 1/3 cup of bone broth
- 1 tablespoon freshly squeezed orange juice
- 1 Serrano pepper, deveined and chopped
- 1 sweet bell pepper, deveined and chopped
- 1/2 teaspoon fennel seeds

COOKING STEPS

1. Rinse and dry the pork; season it with salt. Then, preheat a non-stick skillet over a moderate flame and heat the oil.

2. Sear the pork in hot oil on all sides; cook until browned and transfer to the Instant Pot. Now, add the rest of the above ingredients.

3. Cook using HIGH pressure for 50 minutes. When cooking is complete, use a quick release. After that, release any remaining steam.

4. Check the meat for doneness and let it cool slightly before pulling apart with two forks or shredder claws. Serve warm with steamed peas. Bon appétit!

47. BREAKFAST SAUSAGE WITH TOMATO AND CHILI CHUTNEY

 6 Servings

 Ready in about 1 hour 10 minutes

PER SERVING: 412 Calories; 23.9g Fat; 32.1g Carbs; 16.1g Protein; 27.2g Sugars

Breakfast sausages are mildly spiced pork sausages so that we will use this tomato and chili chutney to enhance the flavors and encourage creativity with the Instant Pot. You don't have to use the whole amount of this chutney; you can keep it in a glass jar for 6 weeks.

INGREDIENTS

- 1 tablespoon lard
- 4 breakfast sausages
- 1 cup water
- 1 tablespoon Italian herbs
- 1 teaspoon garlic flakes
- Garlic salt and freshly ground black pepper, to your liking
- 1 tablespoon corn flour

For Tomato and Chili Chutney:

- 2 small-sized red onions, finely chopped
- 1 pound fresh tomatoes, chopped
- 3 garlic cloves, finely sliced
- 6 fresh red chilies, coarsely chopped
- 1 cup brown sugar
- 1 cup red wine vinegar
- 1 teaspoon paprika
- A few dashes of allspice

COOKING STEPS

1. Start by preheating the Instant Pot on "Sauté" mode and warm the lard. Cook the sausages in the hot lard on all sides. Reserve, keeping warm.

2. Then, make your chutney by mixing all chutney ingredients in a large-sized pan; bring to a simmer, stirring periodically.

3. Let it simmer for 55 minutes to 1 hour on medium-low flame; bring briefly to a boil and remove from the heat.

4. Puree the ingredients using an immersion blender. Add the chutney, along with the water, Italian herbs, garlic flakes, salt and black pepper, to the Instant Pot.

5. Secure the lid and choose "Manual" setting; pressure cook for 8 minutes. Once cooking is complete, perform a quick release.

6. Then, make the slurry by mixing the corn flour with 1 tablespoon of cold water; add the slurry to the pot and press the "Sauté" key. Cook until the sauce has thickened and serve right away.

48. PORK-FILLED WONTONS WITH WINE SAUCE

 16 Servings

 Ready in about 30 minutes

PER SERVING:
305 Calories; 3.1g Fat; 52.5g Carbs; 15.5g Protein; 5.2g Sugars

Wonton wrappers are probably one of the most convenient and versatile foods to cook. These wontons are filled with fantastic ground meat mixture and pressure cooked to golden perfection. Fast, easy and delicious!

INGREDIENTS

- 1 tablespoon olive oil
- 1/2 shallot, finely chopped
- 2 bell pepper, chopped
- 1 pound ground pork
- 1/4 cup of vegetable stock
- 2 tablespoons vermouth
- 1 tablespoon cornstarch
- 1 tablespoon oyster sauce
- Salt and ground black pepper, to taste
- Cayenne pepper, to taste
- A pinch of ground allspice
- 1 teaspoon garlic flakes
- 40 wonton wrappers

For the Sauce:

- 1/3 cup of water
- 1/3 cup of balsamic vinegar
- 1/3 cup white sugar
- 1/3 cup tomato sauce
- 1 tablespoon corn flour, dissolved in 1 tablespoon water

COOKING STEPS

1. Click the "Sauté" button and warm the olive oil until hot; now, sauté the shallot, bell pepper, and pork until the meat is no longer pink; crumble the browned meat with a fork.

2. Add the vegetable stock and vermouth to scrape any brown bits off the bottom of the cooker. Cook for a few minutes more. Add the cornstarch, oyster sauce, salt, black pepper, cayenne pepper, allspice, and garlic flakes to the inner pot.

3. Place about 1 tablespoon of the pork in the middle of a wonton wrapper. Fold the wrapper in half and press the two sides together; seal the edges using an egg wash or a bit of water.

4. Repeat with the other ingredients; just make sure that there are no air pockets in your wontons.

5. Prepare the Instant Pot by adding a steamer rack and 1 cup of water. Place the wontons on the steamer rack, close and lock the lead, and cook at HIGH pressure for about 4 minutes; work in batches. Afterward, perform a quick release.

6. Meanwhile, whisk all the ingredients for the sauce in a saucepan, bringing to a gentle boil. Serve immediately with wontons. Bon appétit!

49. COUNTRY-STYLE PORK AND PORCINI STEW

 6 Servings

 Ready in about 45 minutes

PER SERVING: 273 Calories; 3.5g Fat; 19.7g Carbs; 32.6g Protein; 0.6g Sugars

Flavorful pork side ribs are made incredibly tender thanks to the magic of pressure cooking. Porcini mushrooms add creamed and rich texture to this hearty stew.

INGREDIENTS

- 1 ½ pounds pork side rib
- 10 ounces porcini mushrooms, thinly sliced
- 1 cup carrots coins
- 1/2 cup parsnip, thinly sliced
- 2 bay leaves
- 1/2 teaspoon marjoram
- 3/4 teaspoon sea salt
- 1/2 teaspoon black pepper, preferably freshly ground
- 1 teaspoon smoked cayenne pepper
- 1 teaspoon mustard seeds
- 2 cups of water
- 2 cups of bone broth

COOKING STEPS

1. Simply place all of the above ingredients into the inner pot of your Instant Pot.

2. Press the "Meat/Stew" button; set the timer for 40 minutes.

3. Once cooking is complete, allow the pressure to come down naturally and serve warm. Bon appétit!

50. STICKY MAPLE PORK TENDERLOIN WITH APPLES

 6 Servings

 Ready in about 35 minutes

PER SERVING:
245 Calories; 4.7g Fat; 20.0g Carbs; 30.4g Protein; 15.7g Sugars

This recipe might earn a permanent spot in your next menu planning simply because it is so delicious, easy to make and nutritious. You can substitute honey for maple syrup if desired.

INGREDIENTS

- 1 ½ pounds pork tenderloin
- Kosher salt and freshly ground black pepper, to taste
- 1/4 teaspoon cayenne pepper
- 1 tablespoon wholegrain mustard
- 2 cooking apples, cored and diced
- 1 clove garlic, crushed
- 1/4 cup maple syrup
- 1 tablespoon white wine vinegar
- 1/4 teaspoon grated fresh ginger
- 1/2 teaspoon ground allspice
- 1 teaspoon ground coriander

COOKING STEPS

1. Start by preheating your Instant Pot on "Sauté" setting.

2. Season the pork tenderloin with salt, black pepper, and cayenne pepper; now; rub it with mustard and sear in the Instant Pot until just browned on all sides.

3. Next, add the apples and continue sautéing for 3 to 4 minutes more or until they start to soften.

4. In a small-sized mixing dish, whisk the remaining ingredients. Ladle over pork and apples.

5. Now, choose "Manual" mode and pressure cook for 20 minutes. Allow the pot to release pressure naturally, and carefully remove the lid. Slice the meat and serve immediately.

51. MUSTARD PORK CUTLETS WITH GREEN ONIONS

 6 Servings

 Ready in about 20 minutes + marinating time

PER SERVING:
265 Calories; 7.8g Fat; 6.3g Carbs; 40.6g Protein; 4.9g Sugars

These pork cutlets are one of the tastiest that you can prepare in a pressure cooker. You can thicken the cooking liquid by making the slurry with cornstarch and cold water.

INGREDIENTS

- 6 bone-in pork cutlets
- 2 tablespoons brown mustard
- 1 teaspoon sea salt
- 1/2 teaspoon ground black pepper
- 1 tablespoon soy sauce
- 1 tablespoon olive oil
- 1 teaspoon fresh lemon juice
- 2 cloves garlic, pressed
- 1 tablespoon brown sugar
- 1 cup green onions, sliced
- 1/2 cup bone broth
- 1 tablespoon honey

COOKING STEPS

1. Marinate the pork cutlets with brown mustard, salt, pepper, soy sauce, olive oil, lemon juice, garlic, and sugar for 1 to 2 hours.

2. Now, preheat your Instant Pot on "Sauté" mode. Once hot, discard the marinade and sear the pork cutlets for 2 minutes; flip them over and cook for 2 minutes on the other side. Reserve.

3. Add the green onions and sauté them in pan drippings for 1 to 2 minutes or until start to soften. Slowly and gradually, add bone broth to deglaze the bottom of the cooker.

4. Add honey along with the reserved pork and the remaining marinade.

5. Place the browned pork chops back into the pressure cooker. Close and lock the lid and cook at HIGH Pressure for 5 minutes. Once cooking is complete, allow the pressure to drop naturally. Bon appétit!

52. BEER-BRAISED PORK BUTT

 4 Servings

 Ready in about 55 minutes

PER SERVING:
415 Calories; 24.0 Fat; 17.2g Carbs; 30.1 Protein; 8.7 Sugars

Be generous with the seasonings in this recipe. You can experiment here because it is hard to fail! Here are some ideas: paprika, cumin, mustard seeds, rosemary, seasoned salt, onion powder, ground cloves… The possibilities are endless!

INGREDIENTS

- 1 ½ tablespoons peanut oil
- 1 pound Boston butt
- 1 teaspoon sea salt flakes
- 1/4 teaspoon pink peppercorns, freshly cracked
- 1 teaspoon Mexican oregano
- 3/4 cup shallots, chopped
- 2 garlic cloves, minced
- A pinch of ground allspice
- 1 thyme sprig, only leaves crushed
- 6 ounces beer
- 1 tablespoon balsamic vinegar
- 2 tablespoons honey

COOKING STEPS

1. Start by preheating your Instant Pot on "Sauté" setting and add peanut oil. Season the Boston butt with salt flakes, peppercorns, and Mexican oregano. Then, sear the meat in hot oil until just browned on all sides. Reserve.

2. Add the shallots, garlic, allspice, and thyme and cook for about 1 minute 20 seconds. Add beer and stir continuously, scraping any brown bits off the bottom of the inner pot.

3. Add the reserved pork along with balsamic vinegar and honey. Secure the lid according to the manufacturer's directions. Cook for 50 minutes at HIGH pressure. Once the cooking is complete, allow the pressure to come down by itself.

4. Click the "Sauté" button and evaporate the cooking liquid to get a thicker consistency. Bon appétit!

53. TENDER FESTIVE SIRLOIN STEAK

 6 Servings

 Ready in about 35 minutes

PER SERVING:
289 Calories; 9.3 Fat; 1.9g Carbs; 40.0g Protein; 0.5g Sugars

Pork meat cooks up perfectly in the Instant Pot, while wine and seasonings make this a holiday season must. The trick is in an excellent marinade.

INGREDIENTS

- 2 pounds pork sirloin steak
- 1 teaspoon celery seeds
- 1 teaspoon fine sea salt
- 1/2 teaspoon ground black pepper, or more to taste
- 1 teaspoon cayenne pepper
- 1 teaspoon onion flakes
- 1 ½ tablespoons soy sauce
- 1 tablespoon balsamic vinegar
- 2 tablespoons butter, softened
- 1 cup dry white wine
- 1 cup bone broth
- A few dashes of liquid smoke

COOKING STEPS

1. Mix the first eight ingredients in a large-sized bowl; let them marinate for about 30 minutes.

2. Then, preheat your Instant Pot using the "Sauté" button. Now, melt the butter and brown your pork for 3 minutes on each side.

3. Add the remaining ingredients and stir to combine well.

4. After that, secure the lid and choose "Meat/Stew" setting. Once cooking is complete, allow the pressure to come down naturally. Serve immediately over mashed potatoes. Enjoy!

54. ITALIAN-STYLE PORK RIB AND PANCETTA SOUP

 6 Servings

 Ready in about 50 minutes

PER SERVING:
246 Calories; 15.1g Fat; 7.5g Carbs; 20.0g Protein; 3.9g Sugars

It's cold outside and you are craving a warm and comforting meal. It's soup time! The recipe calls for fennel bulb that you can find all year round. For this recipe, pick the smaller, young bulbs if possible.

INGREDIENTS

- 2 ounces pancetta, finely diced
- 1 onion, chopped
- 1/2 teaspoon crushed red pepper
- 1/2 fennel bulb, cored and diced
- 1 large-sized carrot, chopped
- 1 teaspoon kosher salt
- 2 bay leaves
- 3/4 pound country ribs
- 1 tablespoon Italian seasonings
- 1 teaspoon cumin powder
- 3/4 teaspoon garlic flakes
- 1 (14-ounce) can plum tomatoes, crushed
- 1 cup bone broth or chicken stock
- 3 cups of water

COOKING STEPS

1. Click the "Sauté" button to heat up your Instant Pot. Now, cook pancetta until crisp; add the onion, crushed red pepper, fennel and carrot and cook until the vegetables are just tender.

2. Now, add the remaining ingredients and close the lid tightly; choose "Soup" mode; cook for 35 to 40 minutes.

3. When the timer goes off, release the pressure naturally. Debone the meat and return it back to the pot.

4. Serve garnished with a dollop of pesto. Bon appétit!

55. WHISKEY PORK STEW WITH GREEN BEANS

 6 Servings

 Ready in about 50 minutes

PER SERVING:
389 Calories; 24.5g Fat; 9.8 Carbs; 27.7g Protein; 1.8g Sugars

Pork shoulder usually takes many hours to be cooked, but the Instant Pot changes all of that. The pork falls apart into the cooking liquid and the green beans add both nutrients and extra flavor.

INGREDIENTS

- 1 teaspoon butter, at room temperature
- 1 ½ pounds pork shoulder, cut into 2 inch chunks
- 1 tablespoon curry powder
- 2 ½ tablespoons whiskey
- 1 tablespoon balsamic vinegar
- 1 celery rib, chopped
- 2 yellow potatoes, peeled and diced
- 2 carrots, trimmed and sliced
- 1/2 tablespoon sea salt
- 1/4 teaspoon black pepper, ground
- 1 teaspoon garlic flakes
- 1 teaspoon cayenne pepper
- 1/2 teaspoon ground cloves
- 2 cups of vegetable stock
- 1 cup of water
- 1 cup green beans, diced

COOKING STEPS

1. Preheat your Instant Pot on "Sauté" setting and add the butter at room temperature. Once melted, briefly sear the pork chunks until just browned.

2. Add the other ingredients without the green beans, to the inner pot of your electric pressure cooker. Secure the lid according to the manual.

3. Choose "Meat/Stew" setting, and cook for approximately 40 minutes. Once cooking is complete, perform a quick release.

4. Stir in the green beans and program the cooker back to "Sauté" function; let it simmer for approximately 7 minutes. Serve warm with enough homemade crusty bread. Bon appétit!

56. OLD-FASHIONED PORK LASAGNA

 10 Servings

 Ready in about 40 minutes

PER SERVING: 407 Calories; 21.2g Fat; 31.3g Carbs; 25.5g Protein; 12.3g Sugars

Why it's worth waiting for this lasagna? Because this lasagna feeds a crowd and it always turns out perfect. Serve with a good Italian wine such as Sangiovese.

INGREDIENTS

- 1 pound ground pork
- 1 onion, peeled and chopped
- 1 teaspoon brown sugar
- 2-3 fresh gloves garlic, peeled and finely minced
- 1 sweet bell pepper, deveined and chopped
- 1 ½ teaspoons dried basil leaves
- 1 teaspoon rosemary, fresh or dried
- 1 teaspoon fine sea salt
- 1/4 teaspoon ground black pepper, or more to taste
- Cayenne pepper, to your liking
- 1 teaspoon beef bouillon powder, dissolved in small amount of water
- 10 dry lasagna noodles
- 1 (28-ounce) can crushed tomatoes
- 1 (18-ounce) can tomato paste
- 16 ounces cream cheese
- 1 bunch fresh parsley, roughly chopped
- 3/4 pound mozzarella cheese, sliced
- 3/4 cup grated Parmesan cheese

COOKING STEPS

1. Preheat your Instant Pot on "Sauté" mode and cook the first 10 items until the meat is no longer pink and the onion is translucent and fragrant. Use the beef bouillon to deglaze the pot. Reserve.

2. Spritz a heat-proof dish with non-stick cooking oil. Then, cook lasagna noodles in boiling water for about 10 minutes; drain the noodles.

3. To assemble your lasagna, arrange 4 to 6 noodles lengthwise over the bottom of the baking dish. In a mixing dish, thoroughly whisk the canned tomatoes, tomato paste, cream cheese, and parsley.

4. Now, place the cheese-tomato layer over the noodles. Add a layer of meat mixture. Then, spread mozzarella over it.

5. Top with lasagna noodles. Repeat the layers twice and top with grated Parmesan cheese.

6. Cover with foil to prevent burning. Insert a trivet into your Instant Pot; add 1 ½ cups of water to the base of the pot.

7. Turn to "Manual" function and cook for 20 minutes at HIGH pressure. Afterward, perform a natural release. Bon appétit!

57. PORK CHOPS WITH PEAR AND GINGER SAUCE

 4 Servings

 Ready in about 15 minutes

PER SERVING:
409 Calories; 28.6g Fat; 18.5g Carbs; 19.9g Protein; 11.2g Sugars

Enjoy this perfectly cooked pork chops in sweet and tangy pear sauce. Serve alongside a fresh salad, corn on the cob or steamed green beans.

INGREDIENTS

- 1 ½ tablespoons olive oil
- 4 pork sirloin chops
- Fine sea salt and freshly ground black pepper, to your liking
- 1/2 teaspoon red pepper flakes, crushed
- 4 cloves garlic, roughly minced
- 1 shallot, peeled and sliced
- 2 Anjou pears, peeled, cored and sliced
- 1-inch piece of fresh ginger, peeled and grated
- 3 tablespoons cider vinegar
- 1 teaspoon ground allspice
- 1 cup bone broth
- 1 tablespoon Worcestershire sauce

COOKING STEPS

1. Start by preheating your Instant Pot on "Sauté" mode; heat the olive oil.

2. Season the pork with salt, black pepper, and red pepper. Now, sear the meat for 3 minutes on each side. Reserve.

3. Then, sauté the garlic and shallot in the pan drippings; cook until tender and translucent.

4. Now, add the pears, ginger, vinegar, allspice, broth, and Worcestershire sauce; stir with a wooden spatula scraping any brown bits off the bottom of the inner pot.

5. Add the pork chops back to the pot. Secure the lid and cook at HIGH pressure for 1 minute. Lastly, use a natural release and remove the lid according to the manual.

6. Finally, you can thicken the sauce with a mix of corn flour and water; use "Sauté" mode. Serve warm.

58. FINGER LICKIN' PORK ROAST WITH PINEAPPLE

 6 Servings

 Ready in about 40 minutes

PER SERVING: 445 Calories; 20.0g Fat; 16.3g Carbs; 47.8g Protein; 12.3g Sugars

Blade roast is brilliant in its simplicity and it cooks easily and effortlessly in the Instant Pot. However, we added pineapple rings for fruity and fancy flavor. Enjoy the feast!

INGREDIENTS

- 2 pounds blade roast, trimmed of excess fat
- 1 cup orange juice
- 1 tablespoon sugar
- Sea salt flakes and freshly cracked mixed peppercorns, to taste
- 2-3 whole cloves
- 1/4 cup of light soy sauce
- 1 tablespoon finely grated fresh ginger
- 1 can pineapple rings, juice reserved
- 1/2 cup scallions
- 1/2 teaspoon dried dill weed
- Roughly chopped coriander leaves, to serve

COOKING STEPS

1. Put the pork, orange juice, sugar, salt, peppercorns, and the cloves into the Instant Pot. Secure the lid.

2. Press "Meat/Stew" key and pressure cook for 33 minutes; when the cooking is complete, use a natural release.

3. Add the soy sauce, ginger, pineapple, scallions, and dill; stir and secure the lid again. Let it cook on "Manual" for 5 minutes. Once cooking is complete, use a quick release.

4. Garnish with fresh coriander and serve over warm rice.

59. GRANDMA'S PORK AND SAUSAGE CABBAGE ROLLS

 16 Servings

 Ready in about 40 minutes

PER SERVING:
202 Calories; 9.1g Fat; 14.2g Carbs; 15.7g Protein; 3.1g Sugars

This all-star recipe is an integral part of every home cookbook worldwide. However, every great-grandmother has her own twist on this classic dish. For instance, a homemade roasted tomato paste works well for the sauce. Enjoy!

INGREDIENTS

- 1 head white cabbage

For the Filling:
- 3 cloves garlic, finely minced
- 3/4 cup shallots, chopped
- Sea salt flakes, to taste
- 1/4 teaspoon freshly cracked black pepper
- 1/3 teaspoon smoked cayenne pepper
- 2 tablespoons minced fresh parsley leaves
- 1 ¼ pounds ground pork
- 3/4 pound Kielbasa sausage, removed from casings and chopped
- 3/4 cup brown rice, cooked

For the Sauce:
- 1 ½ tablespoons olive oil
- 3/4 cup yellow onion, peeled and finely chopped
- 2 teaspoons garlic paste
- 1 cup of chicken broth
- 2 (14.5-ounce) cans diced tomatoes with their juice
- 1/3 cup cider vinegar
- 1/2 teaspoon cumin powder
- A pinch of grated nutmeg
- Salt, to taste
- 5-6 black peppercorns
- 1 tablespoon cornstarch, dissolved in 1 ½ tablespoons cold water

COOKING STEPS

1. Cook the cabbage in boiling water for about 8 minutes or until outer leaves loosen from the head. Remove the outer leaves and set them aside. Return the cabbage to the boiling water and repeat until all leaves are softened; discard tough center stalk from each leaf.

2. Set aside 16 large leaves for rolls; chop the remaining cabbage.

3. Meanwhile, heat up your cooker on "Sauté" mode. Stir in all filling ingredients but not the rice; sauté until the pork Kielbasa is no longer pink. Now, stir in the rice and cook until everything is heated through.

4. To make the sauce, heat the oil in a deep saucepan. Then, sauté the onion until just tender and translucent; add the garlic paste and stir just 30 seconds longer.

5. Stir in the chicken broth, tomatoes, cider vinegar, cumin, nutmeg and salt; bringing to a gentle boil; add 1/2 cup of the chopped cabbage.

6. Then, assemble your rolls. Divide the filling among the prepared cabbage leaves. Fold in sides and roll up the cabbage leaf to enclose the filling mixture.

7. Add the rack and 1 cup of water to the Instant Pot. Place 8 cabbage rolls, seam side down, on the rack. Add about 1/2 of the sauce.

8. Place another 8 rolls over it; top with the remaining sauce and scatter black peppercorns over everything; cook in batches, if necessary.

9. Then, secure the lid in place, and cook for 18 minutes at HIGH pressure. Once the cooking is done, perform a quick release. Transfer the cabbage rolls to a serving platter.

10. Select "Sauté" and cook the sauce bringing to a gentle boil. To thicken the sauce, add the cornstarch slurry, stirring frequently to avoid lumps. Pour the sauce over the cabbage rolls and serve immediately.

60. FASTER-THAN-FAST-FOOD PORK RIBS

 6 Servings

 Ready in about 25 minutes

PER SERVING: 379 Calories; 21.0g Fat; 19.3g Carbs; 26.8g Protein; 12.5g Sugars

The Instant Pot is your little kitchen "helper" during the holiday season while the oven is occupied with other dishes. Therefore, these barbecue ribs are perfectly fit into a holiday menu plan!

INGREDIENTS

- 2 1/3 pounds baby back pork ribs
- 1 teaspoon sea salt flakes
- 1/4 teaspoon freshly ground black pepper, or more to taste
- 1 teaspoon smoked paprika
- 1 tablespoon garlic, paste
- 1 ½ tablespoons butter
- 1 tablespoon chili powder
- 1/2 cup bone broth
- 1 cup barbeque sauce
- 1 tablespoon brown sugar
- 1 tablespoon Worcester sauce
- 1/2 teaspoon onion powder
- 1 tablespoon cornstarch, dissolved in 1 ½ tablespoons of water

COOKING STEPS

1. Season the pork ribs with the salt flakes, black pepper, and paprika; then rub them with garlic paste. Push the "Sauté" button and melt the butter. Then, brown the pork ribs and reserve them.

2. Add the chili powder, broth, barbecue sauce, sugar, Worcester sauce and onion powder; stir until heated through. Secure the lid in and cook for 18 minutes at HIGH pressure.

3. Afterward, perform a natural pressure release; remove the cooker's lid.

4. Select "Sauté" program to thicken the cooking juices; add the cornstarch slurry and cook until the liquid has reduced by half.

5. Add the pork ribs back, gently stir to combine, and serve. Bon appétit!

BEEF RECIPES

61. VEGGIE AND GROUND BEEF CHUNKY SOUP

 6 Servings

 Ready in about 20 minutes

PER SERVING:
231 Calories; 7.6 Fat; 21.8g Carbs; 20.9g Protein; 5.9g Sugars

This warming meaty soup is a perfect idea on a cold winter day; it will definitely nourish your body and soul. Serve with enough cornbread.

INGREDIENTS

- 1 ½ tablespoons butter
- 1 cup scallions, chopped
- 1 carrot, chopped
- 2 parsnips, chopped
- 2 cloves garlic, minced
- 3/4 pound ground beef
- 1/2 teaspoon sea salt
- 1/2 teaspoon ground black pepper, or more to taste
- 1 bay leaf
- 3 ½ cups roasted vegetable stock
- 1 bottle tomato-vegetable juice cocktail
- 1 (15-ounce) can whole kernel corn, drained
- 1 cup frozen kale leaves, torn into small pieces

COOKING STEPS

1. Heat up your Instant Pot on "Sauté" setting; now, melt the butter and cook the scallions, carrot, parsnip, and garlic until just tender.

2. After that, add ground beef, salt, pepper, and bay leaf and cook until the beef is no longer pink; crumble with a fork.

3. Pour in beef broth to deglaze the bottom of your cooker; stir in the remaining ingredients. Secure the lid, choose the "Manual" button and cook for 5 minutes at HIGH pressure.

4. Once cooking is complete, use a quick pressure release. Stir in corn and kale; stir until they are thoroughly heated. Bon appétit!

62. FAMILY FAVORITE BEEF STEW WITH GREEN PEAS

 8 Servings

 Ready in about 55 minutes

PER SERVING:
223 Calories; 5.6g Fat; 14.4g Carbs; 28.1g Protein; 3.4g Sugars

If you have friends coming over, this hearty stew should be on the menu! Serve with homemade cornbread or croutons. Enjoy!

INGREDIENTS

- 1 ½ pounds pot roast, cut into cubes
- 1 ½ cups bone broth
- 2 cups water
- 1 leek, chopped
- 2 fennel bulbs, chopped
- 2 carrots, chopped
- 1 parsnip, chopped
- 1 teaspoon salt
- 1/4 teaspoon ground black pepper
- 1/4 teaspoon turmeric powder
- 1/2 teaspoon dried dill weed
- 1/4 teaspoon grated fresh ginger root
- 1 cup green peas

COOKING STEPS

1. Place the pot roast, bone broth, and water into the Instant Pot; close and lock the lid and press the "Manual" key. Cook for 40 minutes at HIGH pressure.

2. Once cooking is complete, release the pressure manually; carefully remove the lid. Add the leek, fennel bulbs, carrots, parsnip, and seasonings.

3. Program it back to "Manual" function and pressure cook for 10 minutes. Then, release the pressure and carefully remove the lid; add green peas, stir, and press "Keep Warm/Cancel" button.

4. Add the seasonings and serve in individual bowls. Bon appétit!

63. PENNE WITH SHORT RIBS AND TOMATO SAUCE

 6 Servings

 Ready in about 25 minutes

PER SERVING: 550 Calories; 14.4g Fat; 43.9g Carbs; 58.7g Protein; 12.7g Sugars

Select top-notch ribs and make this rich and satisfying meal for your family and friends. With a light and flavorful fresh tomato sauce, these spare ribs are addictive!

INGREDIENTS

- 1 ½ tablespoons lard
- 1 cup leeks, thinly sliced
- 3 garlic cloves, minced
- 1 carrot, cleaned and chopped
- 1/3 cup tomato paste
- 1/4 cup honey
- 1/4 cup malt vinegar
- 1/2 teaspoon allspice
- 3 cups fresh ripe tomatoes, chopped
- 1 teaspoon turmeric powder
- 1 teaspoon powdered mustard
- 1 teaspoon cayenne pepper
- 1/2 teaspoon salt
- 1/4 teaspoon ground black pepper, or more to taste
- 3 pounds beef short spare ribs, cut into small pieces
- 2 tablespoons cornstarch slurry
- Cooked penne, to serve

COOKING STEPS

1. Begin by preheating your cooker on "Sauté" mode and warm the lard; sauté the leeks until they start to soften; add minced garlic and stir until aromatic and just browned.

2. Stir in the other ingredients, minus cornstarch slurry and penne.

3. Choose "Meat/Stew" setting and pressure cook for 15 minutes. Allow the pressure to come down on its own and carefully open the cooker following the manufacturer's instructions.

4. Afterwards, add the cornstarch slurry to thicken the tomato sauce. Serve with cooked penne. Enjoy!

64. SPICY SOUTHWESTERN MEATLOAF

 6 Servings

 Ready in about 35 minutes

PER SERVING: 356 Calories; 10.4g Fat; 30.6g Carbs; 34.5g Protein; 7.2g Sugars

You won't go wrong with this meatloaf! Simply mix all ingredients for the meat mixture, shape them into a loaf and cover it with tomato sauce; and in under 30 minutes sit down to a delicious slice of meatloaf!

INGREDIENTS

- 1 tablespoon olive oil
- 1 shallot, peeled and chopped
- 2 cloves garlic, finely minced
- 1 parsnip, chopped
- 1 celery stalk, chopped
- 1 carrots, grated
- 2 green chilies, minced
- 1 cup baked corn tortilla chips, crushed
- 1 ¼ teaspoons kosher salt
- 1/3 teaspoon ground black pepper, or more to taste
- 1/3 cup minced flat-leaf parsley
- 1/3 cup milk
- 1 large-sized egg, beaten
- 1 ¼ pounds beef, ground
- 1 cup tomato sauce
- 1 tablespoon brown sugar
- A few dashes of Tabasco, optional

COOKING STEPS

1. Firstly, preheat a nonstick skillet over a moderate flame; now, heat the oil. Quickly cook the shallot and garlic in the hot oil, moving them around the skillet using a wooden spoon.

2. Add the parsnip, celery, carrot, and green chilies; cook until they begin to soften. Transfer them to a large-sized mixing dish.

3. Stir in crushed tortilla chips, salt, pepper, parsley, milk, egg, and beef; mix until everything is well incorporated.

4. Shape the mixture into a meatloaf; add 1 ½ cups water to the base of the Instant Pot. Insert a steamer rack into the pot. Spritz the foil with a nonstick cooking spray. Place the shaped meatloaf in the foil; lower it onto the steamer rack.

5. In a mixing bowl, whisk tomato sauce, sugar, and Tabasco (optional). Pour the tomato sauce over the top of the meatloaf.

6. Secure the lid and choose "Manual" setting; cook at HIGH pressure for 23 minutes. Serve warm with Tex-mex mashers if desired.

65. WINTER POT ROAST WITH ROOT VEGETABLES

 6 Servings

 Ready in about 1 hour 10 minutes

PER SERVING: 358 Calories; 12.7g Fat; 9.1g Carbs; 47.8g Protein; 1.6g Sugars

Firstly, brown the beef to seal the natural juices and flavors before starting pressure cooking. Make sure to include dried and fresh seasonings, which give the pot roast a spicy boost for cold winter days.

INGREDIENTS

- 2 pounds pot roast
- Salt and pepper, to your liking
- 1 ½ tablespoons softened butter
- 1 cup scallions, chopped
- 3 cloves garlic, minced
- 1 celery stalk, chopped
- 1 celery rib, chopped
- 1 large-sized carrot, cleaned and chopped
- 1 fennel bulb, sliced
- 2 tablespoons oyster sauce
- 1 bay leaf
- 1 teaspoon dried marjoram
- 1/4 cup dry vermouth
- 3/4 cup bone broth
- 1/3 teaspoon cumin powder
- 1 ½ tablespoons cornstarch, dissolved in 2 tablespoons
- 1 tablespoon fresh basil

COOKING STEPS

1. Heat up your Instant Pot on "Sauté" function. Generously season the beef with the salt and pepper on all sides.

2. Then, melt the butter and sear the seasoned beef for about 8 minutes; flip it and cook on the other side for additional 8 to 10 minutes. Set aside.

3. Then, in the pan drippings, sauté the scallions until tender; add the garlic and cook, stirring frequently, for 30 to 40 seconds more.

4. After that, stir in the celery, carrot, fennel bulb, oyster sauce, bay leaf, and dried marjoram and continue sautéing for 5 minutes more or until they are tender; you can add the broth, one spoon at a time, to prevent veggies from sticking to the bottom. Reserve the sautéed vegetables.

5. Now, add the beef back to the pot; add the remaining bone broth, vermouth, and cumin, and secure the lid. Cook for 40 minutes at HIGH pressure. Once cooking is done, release the pressure using a quick release method. Open the lid carefully.

6. Add the prepared cornstarch slurry to the cooking juice and stir until the sauce has thickened. Serve garnished with fresh basil. Enjoy!

66. MOUTH-WATERING CHIPOLATA SAUSAGE CASSEROLE

 6 Servings

 Ready in about 15 minutes

PER SERVING:
343 Calories; 11.0g Fat; 26.3g Carbs; 34.7g Protein; 13.9g Sugars

This sausage casserole is so simple to make in the Instant Pot, but it has rich flavors of beef chipolata sausages, fresh and dried herbs, and Pepper Jack cheese. Enjoy!

INGREDIENTS

- 1 ¼ pounds lean beef chipolata sausages
- 3 cloves garlic, finely minced
- 1 yellow onion, peeled and finely chopped
- 1 tablespoon fresh roughly chopped parsley
- 1 bell pepper, deveined and chopped
- 1 (14.5-ounce) can diced tomatoes, with juices
- 1 cup tomato ketchup
- 1/4 cup apple cider
- 1/4 cup roasted vegetable stock
- 1/3 cup Arborio rice
- 1 tablespoon oyster sauce
- Fine sea salt and ground black pepper, to taste
- 1/2 teaspoon cayenne pepper
- 1 teaspoon dried saffron
- 1 teaspoon dried thyme
- 3/4 cup Pepper Jack cheese, grated

COOKING STEPS

1. Start by preheating your Instant Pot on "Sauté" mode. Now, brown the chipolata sausages along with the garlic and onion until it is no longer pink.

2. Stir in the other ingredients, minus Pepper Jack cheese. Secure the cooker's lid and adjust the timer for 5 minutes. Cook at HIGH pressure.

3. When time is up, allow the pressure to come down on its own and carefully remove the cooker's lid.

4. Transfer the mixture to an oven-proof dish. Top with cheese and bake in the preheated oven until the cheese is bubbly. Bon appétit!

67. BRAISED BEEF SHANK WITH VEGETABLES

 8 Servings

 Ready in about 50 minutes

PER SERVING:
344 Calories; 9.6g Fat; 5.9g Carbs; 50.3g Protein; 2.2g Sugars

You can serve these tender beef shanks over mashed potatoes, but they will also be a good match with pasta or rice. If you don't have button mushrooms, use any kind of white mushrooms you have on hand.

INGREDIENTS

- 2 ½ pounds beef shanks
- Fine sea salt flakes, to your liking
- 1 medium-sized leek, quartered
- 4 garlic cloves
- 1 celery stalk, chopped
- 2 celery ribs, diced
- 2 carrots, thinly sliced
- 6 white button mushrooms, trimmed and quartered
- 2 ½ cups bone broth
- 1 cup red wine
- 1 teaspoon whole mixed peppercorns
- 1/2 teaspoon bay leaf powder
- 1/4 teaspoon cumin powder
- 2 sprigs thyme, chopped

COOKING STEPS

1. Pat the beef dry and generously season it with sea salt flakes. Now, heat up your cooker on "Sauté" setting; sear the meat for about 8 minutes, flipping it over a number of times; reserve.

2. Now, add the leeks and cook for about 5 minutes or until they soften. Then, add the garlic, celery and carrot and cook for a few more minutes or until just tender.

3. Now, stir in the mushrooms and cook for another couple of minutes or until fragrant. Make sure to stir the vegetables frequently.

4. Next, add the remaining ingredients, along with the seared beef.

5. Set the cooker to "Meat/Stew" function; program the timer to 30 minutes. When the time is over, allow the pressure to drop down according to the manual and open the cooker's lid.

68. BEER AND SAGE BEEF BRISKET

 6 Servings

 Ready in about 30 minutes + marinating time

PER SERVING: 283 Calories; 11.1g Fat; 6.4g Carbs; 35.9g Protein; 0.8g Sugars

Beautifully marinated with spices and beer, this beef brisket is rich and juicy – a feast for the eyes and the belly! With a delicious gravy, it makes the ultimate comfort food.

INGREDIENTS

- 1 ½ pounds beef brisket, cubed
- Kosher salt and black pepper, to your liking
- 2 tablespoons fresh lemon juice
- 6 ounces beer
- 2 tablespoons butter
- 1 cup scallions, finely chopped
- 4 cloves garlic, minced
- 1 teaspoon fresh sage, chopped
- 2 tablespoons soy sauce
- 1/2 teaspoon smoked cayenne pepper
- 1 bunch fresh parsley, roughly chopped
- 1 ½ tablespoons cornstarch, dissolved in 2 tablespoons cold water

COOKING STEPS

1. Generously season the beef brisket with salt and pepper; add fresh lemon juice and beer, and marinate in the refrigerator for an hour.

2. Then, heat up your Instant Pot using "Sauté" setting; melt the butter and brown the marinated beef brisket for a few minutes; work in batches. Reserve the meat and cook the scallions in the pan drippings until tender.

3. Add the garlic and sage, and cook for 1 minute more or until aromatic.

4. After that, add the soy sauce, cayenne pepper, and parsley. Cook for 20 minutes.

5. Once the cooking time is over, turn off the Instant Pot and open the lid once the pressure is completely released.

6. Next, stir in the cornstarch slurry. Leave the lid off and choose the "Sauté" setting; bring to a gentle boil, stir and press the "Cancel" button. Bon appétit!

69. HOLIDAY CAJUN PRIME RIB

 4 Servings

 Ready in about 30 minutes

PER SERVING: 225 Calories; 7.6g Fat; 0.9g Carbs; 34.9g Protein; 0.0g Sugars

Prime rib is the king of beef cuts! This simple but effective recipe is all you need to take holiday dinner to the next level. Enjoy!

INGREDIENTS

- 1 pound prime rib, thinly sliced
- 1 teaspoon mustard powder
- 1/3 teaspoon cumin powder
- 1 tablespoon Cajun seasoning
- Salt and pepper, to savor
- 2 tablespoons dry sherry
- 1 ½ cups vegetable stock
- 1 tablespoon fresh chives, minced

COOKING STEPS

1. Firstly, rub the meat with seasonings. Sear the meat on "Sauté" setting until no longer pink.

2. Add dry sherry to deglaze the pot; now, pour in the stock and gently stir to combine.

3. Cook for 20 minutes at HIGH pressure; check the meat for doneness. When time is up, turn off the cooker and remove the lid once the pressure is completely released.

4. Finally, scatter fresh chives over the beef and serve warm with a fresh or pickled salad of choice. Bon appétit!

70. BEEF AND BLACK BEAN CHILI WITH CILANTRO CREAM

 6 Servings

 Ready in about 40 minutes

PER SERVING:
619 Calories; 20.2g Fat; 60.6g Carbs; 49.6g Protein; 7.0g Sugars

INGREDIENTS

- 2 tablespoons peanut oil
- 1 cup red onions, peeled and finely chopped
- 2 cloves garlic, finely minced
- 1 bell pepper, deveined and chopped
- 1 large-sized carrot, chopped
- 1 medium sweet potato, peeled and diced
- 1 ¼ pounds ground beef
- 1/2 teaspoon freshly ground black pepper
- 1 teaspoon kosher salt
- 1 teaspoon Mexican oregano
- 1 tablespoon smoked paprika
- 1 (14.5-ounce) can diced tomatoes in juice, fire-roasted if possible, undrained
- 1 tablespoon packed light brown sugar
- 3 tablespoons sherry vinegar
- 1 teaspoon cocoa powder, unsweetened
- 1 (16-ounce) can black beans, drained and rinsed

For the Cilantro Cream:

- 1 cup sour cream
- 1/3 cup fresh cilantro, minced
- 2 tablespoons freshly squeezed lime juice
- A pinch of salt

The Chile de Árbol is pointed dried red pepper that can be found in the Latin section of the supermarket. Keep in mind that they are extremely hot. Mexican oregano has an earthy fragrance, similar to the Greek oregano, but the Mediterranean one has a stronger flavor.

COOKING STEPS

1. Hit the "Sauté" button and warm the peanut oil. Sauté the onion, garlic, peppers, carrot and sweet potato for approximately 4 minutes or until they are softened.

2. Next, stir in the ground beef and cook for 5 to 6 minutes or until just browned; crumble with a fork.

3. Throw in the seasonings, tomatoes, sugar, vinegar, cocoa powder, and beans. Fasten the lid on the cooker.

4. Now, choose "Bean/Chili" function and pressure cook for 20 minutes. Once the cooking time is over, wait until the Instant Pot depressurizes on its own.

5. To make the cilantro cream, simply mix all the cream ingredients in a small-sized dish. Cover and chill until serving time.

6. Serve your chili in individual bowls dolloped with the cold cilantro cream. Bon appétit!

71. Beef and Locatelli Meatballs in Tomato Sauce

 6 Servings

 Ready in about 25 minutes

PER SERVING: 361 Calories; 15.3g Fat; 20.5g Carbs; 36.2g Protein; 8.9g Sugars

These meatballs are so easy and so delicious that you'll want to cook them all the time! If you have a homemade tomato sauce on hand, you are sure to succeed!

INGREDIENTS

For the Meatballs:
- 1 cup yellow onions, peeled and finely chopped
- 1/2 cup Locatelli cheese, preferably freshly grated
- 1/3 cup breadcrumbs
- 1 teaspoon dried basil
- 1/2 teaspoon marjoram
- Sea salt and black pepper, to taste
- 1 egg, whisked
- 1 ¼ pounds ground beef

For the Sauce:
- 2 tablespoons olive oil
- 1/2 cup onions, chopped
- 2 cloves garlic, minced
- 1 sweet pepper, deveined and chopped
- 1 small-sized celery stalk, cleaned and chopped
- 1 tablespoon fresh parsley
- 3 cups tomato sauce, preferably homemade
- 1 cup vegetable broth
- 1/2 cup water

COOKING STEPS

1. In a mixing dish, thoroughly combine all ingredients for the meatballs. Shape the mixture into meatballs and brown them briefly in a preheated heavy-bottomed skillet. Cook on all sides, moving them around the bottom of skillet constantly. Set aside.

2. After that, preheat your cooker on "Sauté" setting; warm the oil and cook the onions until translucent. Then, stir in the garlic and cook until just browned or about 1 minute; make sure to stir frequently.

3. Add sweet pepper and celery and continue sautéing until they start to soften. Now, add the fresh parsley, tomato sauce, vegetable broth and water; bring it to a boil. Carefully drop the browned meatballs into the sauce.

4. Lock the lid onto the pot and cook for 4 minutes at HIGH pressure. Use the quick-release method to bring the pressure in the pot back to normal. Serve with your favorite pasta.

72. FESTIVE TANGY AND SPICY BEEF SALAD

 6 Servings

 Ready in about 1 hour

PER SERVING: 339 Calories; 14.0g Fat; 14.5g Carbs; 36.8g Protein; 9.0g Sugars

This is one of the simplest beef salad recipes. If you could find pasture-raised beef for this recipe, you will have a completely healthy and nutritious meal.

INGREDIENTS

- 1 ½ pounds sirloin steaks
- 1 cup bone broth
- 1 teaspoon honey
- 1 tablespoon soy sauce
- 1/3 cup sweet chili sauce
- 1/3 cup freshly squeezed lime juice
- 2 tomatoes, finely chopped
- 1 large-sized avocado, peeled, diced
- 1 purple onion, peeled and chopped
- 1 head lettuce, torn into small pieces
- Sea salt flakes and white pepper, to season

COOKING STEPS

1. Lightly grease your Instant Pot with a nonstick cooking spray. Add the sirloin steaks and bone broth. Cook on "Meat/Stew" setting for 40 minutes.

2. Use the quick-release method to bring the pressure back to normal; make sure to release any remaining steam and carefully open the cooker. Set it aside to rest for 5 to 10 minutes before slicing.

3. After that, cut sirloin steaks into thin slices by cutting against the grain.

4. In a mixing bowl, thoroughly whisk the honey, soy sauce, chili sauce, and fresh lime juice; cover and keep in the refrigerator.

5. Next, mix the tomatoes, avocado, onions, and lettuce; season with salt flakes and white pepper to taste. Mound the salad onto individual serving plates. Drizzle with the chilled dressing. Top with beef and serve immediately.

73. SPLIT PEA AND GROUND BEEF SOUP

 6 Servings

 Ready in about 25 minutes

PER SERVING:
310 Calories; 7.8g Fat; 32.3g Carbs; 28.8g Protein; 5.1g Sugars

Healthy, satisfying and economical, split peas are a home cook's favorite. But, there are two tricks – don't overfill the pot and always use a natural release; just allow it to rest a bit after pressure cooking.

INGREDIENTS

- 1 ¼ cups split pea
- 1 ½ tablespoons coconut oil
- 1 cup shallot, chopped
- 1 large-sized carrot, chopped
- 1 parsnip, chopped
- 1 teaspoon garlic paste
- 3/4 pound ground beef
- 1 teaspoon smoked paprika
- 1 teaspoon sea salt flakes
- 1/2 teaspoon ground black pepper
- 1 teaspoon crushed dried thyme
- 2 cups vegetable stock
- 1 cup water
- 2 cups chopped tomatoes

COOKING STEPS

1. Firstly, soak the split pea for 8 to 10 hours or overnight.

2. Then, heat up your Instant Pot on "Sauté" setting; now, melt the coconut oil and cook the shallots, carrot, and parsnip, until they're just tender.

3. After that, add the garlic paste, ground beef, paprika, salt flakes, black pepper, and thyme and cook, stirring continuously, until the beef is no longer pink.

4. Pour in the stock to deglaze the bottom of the pot; add the water and crushed tomatoes. Secure the lid, choose the "Manual" button and cook for 15 minutes at HIGH pressure.

5. Once cooking is complete, use a natural release. Once the cooker returns to normal pressure, carefully and slowly open the lid; stir the soup and serve in individual bowls. Bon appétit!

74. COLORFUL VEGETABLE AND BURGER SOUP

 6 Servings

 Ready in about 35 minutes

PER SERVING: 264 Calories; 5.4g Fat; 45.3g Carbs; 9.9g Protein; 8.3g Sugars

In this recipe, you can use your favorite mixed vegetables too. Keep in mind that they should be frozen. If you have leftover vegetables, don't throw them away, just freeze them for soups and stews.

INGREDIENTS

- 1 tablespoon olive oil
- 1 medium-sized leek, finely chopped
- 1 teaspoon garlic from jar, minced
- 3/4 pound ground sirloin
- 1/4 cup dry wine
- 5 cups roasted vegetable stock
- 2 (14.5-ounce) cans chopped tomatoes
- 2 tablespoons ketchup
- 3/4 cup quick barley
- 1 turnip, chopped
- 1 carrot, chopped
- 2 sweet potatoes, peeled and diced
- 3 cups cauliflower florets
- 1 cup collard
- 1 teaspoon bay leaf powder
- 1 teaspoon of dried thyme
- A pinch of ground allspice
- 1 teaspoon kosher salt
- 1/2 teaspoon ground black pepper

COOKING STEPS

1. Heat up your cooker on "Sauté" mode; now, heat the oil and sauté the leeks until tender; add the garlic and continue sautéing until just tender and aromatic.

2. Now, add the beef and brown it, stirring frequently. Then, pour in dry wine to deglaze the pot. Add the stock, tomatoes, ketchup, and barley. Click the "Soup" button and cook for 10 minutes at HIGH pressure.

3. Use the quick-release method to bring the pot's pressure back to normal. Add the rest of the above ingredients.

4. Program it back to "Soup" function and set the machine's timer to cook at HIGH pressure for 15 minutes. Use the quick release pressure again. Bon appétit!

75. MOM'S SAUCY CHIPOTLE SKIRT STEAK

 8 Servings

 Ready in about 55 minutes

PER SERVING:
264 Calories; 12.2g Fat; 2.7g Carbs; 34.6g Protein; 1.1g Sugars

This is a great dish for a typical weeknight. Serve with Kaiser rolls and spicy horseradish mustard. You might be surprised at how savory this beef is!

INGREDIENTS

- 2 pounds beef skirt steak
- 1/2 teaspoon pink Himalayan salt
- 1/4 teaspoon freshly ground black pepper
- 1 tablespoon rendered bacon fat
- 2 canned chipotles in adobo sauce, stemmed, seeded, and chopped
- 1/4 cup unsweetened apple juice
- 2 tablespoons fresh lime juice
- 1 tablespoon oyster sauce
- 4 juniper berries
- 2 tablespoons extra-virgin olive oil
- 1 tablespoon minced garlic
- 1 bay leaf

COOKING STEPS

1. Season the beef skirt steak with salt and pepper. Then, heat up your cooker using the "Sauté" button. Now, melt bacon fat and sear the seasoned meat on all sides.

2. In a food processor, puree canned chipotles together with apple juice, lime juice, oyster sauce, juniper berries, olive oil, and garlic.

3. Add the pureed sauce, along with bay leaf, to the cooker and lock the lid onto the pot. Using "Manual" function, set the machine's timer to cook at HIGH pressure for 35 minutes.

4. Allow the pressure to fall to normal naturally, about 15 minutes. Unlock and open the lid. Serve warm.

FISH & SEAFOOD

77

80

83

87

90

76. EVERYDAY SHRIMP PILAF WITH PARMIGIANO-REGGIANO

 6 Servings

 Ready in about 35 minutes

PER SERVING: 310 Calories; 6.7g Fat; 40.6g Carbs; 18.9g Protein; 2.2g Sugars

This elegant dish may become your favorite weeknight staple. The rice is soft but a little chewy, while the shrimp is flavorful and delish enough for a festive dinner

INGREDIENTS

- 2 tablespoons olive oil
- 1 cup scallions, chopped
- 3 garlic cloves, finely minced
- 1 jarred roasted red bell pepper, chopped
- 1 1/3 cups medium-grain rice
- 1/4 cup dry sherry
- 3 cups vegetable broth
- 1 cup bottled clam juice
- 1/2 teaspoon ground black pepper
- 1/2 teaspoon cayenne pepper
- Salt, to taste
- 3/4 pound shrimp, peeled and deveined
- 1/2 cup Parmigiano-Reggiano, cheese

COOKING STEPS

1. Start by preheating your Instant Pot on "Sauté" mode; then, warm the olive oil and sauté the scallions until they turn translucent.

2. Now, stir in the garlic and continue sautéing for less than a minute or until aromatic.

3. Add bell pepper and rice; stir over the heat for 1 minute. Pour in the sherry and stir until absorbed, about 2 minutes. Stir in the 1 cup broth and clam juice. Add black pepper, cayenne pepper, and salt.

4. Lock the lid onto the pot. Set the machine to cook at HIGH pressure; set the timer for 10 minutes. Afterwards, perform a quick release to bring the pressure back to normal.

5. Program it back to "Sauté" setting. Now, add the shrimp along with remaining vegetable broth; cook for about 5 minutes.

6. Stir in Parmigiano-Reggiano cheese and serve warm. Bon appétit!

Fish & Seafood | Instant Pot Cookbook

77. CHEESY SALMON PASTA BAKE

 4 Servings

 Ready in about 25 minutes

PER SERVING:
446 Calories; 18.7g Fat; 44.2g Carbs; 25.9g Protein; 3.0g Sugars

Salmon is one of the healthiest foods in the world and it is also very easy to prepare. Under pressure, it becomes flavorful, flaky and mouthwatering.

INGREDIENTS

- 1 ½ tablespoons butter, at room temperature
- 1 shallot, peeled and chopped
- 2 garlic cloves, minced
- 1 small fresh jalapeño chili, stemmed, seeded, and minced
- 10 ounces dry pasta
- 1 1/3 cups water
- 1 (15-ounce) can petite diced tomatoes
- 1/4 teaspoon ground black pepper
- 1/2 teaspoon seasoned salt
- 1 teaspoon dried rosemary
- 1/4 teaspoon dried basil
- 1 teaspoon dried thyme
- 1 can salmon, drained
- 1 cup grated Cheddar cheese
- 1 ½ tablespoons fresh coriander, coarsely chopped

COOKING STEPS

1. Heat up your Instant Pot on "Sauté" program. Melt the butter; now, sauté the shallot, garlic and jalapeño in hot butter until just tender.

2. Stir in the pasta, water, tomatoes, black pepper, salt, rosemary, basil, and thyme. Set the cooker to "Soup" mode and pressure cook for 12 minutes.

3. Use the quick-release method to bring the pot's pressure back to normal. Add salmon and cook uncovered on "Sauté" mode on until heated through.

4. Scrape the mixture into a lightly greased baking dish. Top with Cheddar cheese. Bake in a preheated oven until the cheese is bubbly. Scatter fresh coriander over the top and serve immediately.

78. SHRIMP AND BACON WITH APPLES

 6 Servings

 Ready in about 25 minutes

PER SERVING: 422 Calories; 11.7g Fat; 49.3g Carbs; 29.1g Protein; 10.2g Sugars

This recipe calls for tart green apples such as Granny Smith, which will add some zing to your seafood. However, if you prefer a sweeter sauce, use Gala or Honeycrisp. Further, you can use any kind of canned tomatoes, but fire-roasted diced tomatoes add a rich and char flavor to your dish.

INGREDIENTS

- 1 ½ tablespoons unsalted butter
- 1 leek, white and pale, and thinly sliced
- 3 cloves garlic, crushed
- 1 sweet pepper, seeded and chopped
- 2 tart green apples, peeled, cored, and thinly sliced
- 1 1/3 cups jasmine rice
- 2 tablespoons canned tomato paste
- 1 (14-ounce) can fire-roasted diced tomatoes
- 2 cups vegetable stock, preferably homemade
- 1 bay leaf
- 1 tablespoon oyster sauce
- 1 ½ pounds shrimp, peeled and deveined
- 1 teaspoon dried thyme
- 1/2 teaspoon dried marjoram
- Sea salt flakes and ground black pepper, to your liking
- 1/2 teaspoon smoked cayenne pepper
- 4 thin bacon slices, pre-cooked and chopped

COOKING STEPS

1. Begin by preheating your Instant Pot with the "Sauté" button. Melt the butter and sauté the leek and garlic until tender and aromatic.

2. Stir in the peppers and apples; cook until they begin to soften; it will take less than a minute.

3. Next, stir in the jasmine rice, tomato paste, tomatoes, stock, bay leaf, and oyster sauce. Lock the lid onto the pot. Choose the "Rice" setting. Lastly, use the quick-release method to bring the pressure back to normal and carefully open the cooker.

4. Add the remaining ingredients, secure the lid again, and select "Manual". Set the machine to cook for 3 minutes more. Finally, discard the bay leaf and serve. Bon appétit!

79. CHUNKY SNAPPER AND VEGETABLE SOUP

 8 Servings

 Ready in about 25 minutes

PER SERVING: 245 Calories; 9.9g Fat; 12.7g Carbs; 23.5g Protein; 4.4g Sugars

Steaming the snapper under the intense pressure keeps it moist and flavorful. Sautéed root vegetables are the perfect accompaniment to the fish.

INGREDIENTS

- 1 ½ pounds frozen snapper
- 1/2 teaspoon fine sea salt
- 1/3 teaspoon black peppercorns, freshly ground
- 1 tablespoon olive oil
- 2 garlic cloves, finely minced
- 1 large yellow onion, chopped
- 1 celery stalk, chopped
- 1 celery rib, chopped
- 2 large-sized carrots, chopped
- 1 fennel bulb, chopped
- 1/2 cup dry white wine, such as Chardonnay
- 3/4 cup bottled clam juice
- 2 ½ cups vegetable stock
- 1 tablespoon stemmed fresh thyme leaves
- 1 cup heavy cream
- Thin lemon slices, to serve

COOKING STEPS

1. Add the trivet and 1 cup of water to your pot. Season your fish with salt and black peppercorns; lower onto the trivet.

2. Use the "Manual" function to set the machine's timer to cook at HIGH pressure for 10 minutes. Use the quick-release method to release pressure and open the pot according to the manufacturer's instructions.

3. Transfer the fish with a large, flat spatula from the pot to a cutting board. Cut the fish into bite-sized pieces and set aside, keeping them warm. Clean your pot.

4. Hit the "Sauté" key and warm olive oil; then, sauté the vegetables in hot oil until just tender and fragrant. Pour in the wine to scrape any brown bits off the bottom of the cooker.

5. Pour in clam juice and vegetable stock; add thyme leaves and give it a good stir; secure the cooker's lid. Set the machine's timer to cook for 7 minutes at HIGH pressure. After that, use the quick-release method

6. Now, push the "Sauté" button", add the heavy cream, stir and simmer, uncovered, until it has slightly thickened. Add the fish back to the pot, stir and serve with lemon slices.

80. THE EASIEST FISH CHOWDER EVER

 6 Servings

 Ready in about 25 minutes

PER SERVING:
295 Calories; 17.1g Fat; 6.9g Carbs; 28.3g Protein; 2.2g Sugars

Fish is a staple food in the pressure cooker kitchen, whether for everyday meals or for an impressive holiday fare. This creamy and appetizing chowder is the perfect entree to serve for a lighter festive meal.

INGREDIENTS

- 1 tablespoon butter, at room temperature
- 1 shallot, peeled and chopped
- 4 small green garlic, chopped
- Sea salt and black pepper, to taste
- 1/2 teaspoon smoked paprika
- 1 teaspoon sugar
- 5 cups vegetable broth
- 1/4 cup white wine vinegar
- 1 ½ pounds skin-on fish fillets
- 2 tablespoons fresh dill fronds, chopped
- 2 bay leaves
- 1 ½ cups half-and-half
- 1 tablespoon all-purpose flour
- 1/4 cup chopped fresh chives, to serve

COOKING STEPS

1. Combine the butter, shallot, garlic, salt, black pepper, paprika, and sugar until well mixed.

2. Cook on "Sauté" function for 3 to 4 minutes, stirring frequently. Now, add the broth, wine vinegar, fish, dill, and bay leaves. Lock the lid onto the pot.

3. Set the machine to cook at HIGH pressure for 6 minutes. Use the quick-release method to drop the pot's pressure to normal.

4. Then, thoroughly whisk half-and-half and flour. Add the mixture to the chowder. Push the "Keep Warm/Cancel" button, and simmer for approximately 3 minutes or until it has thickened. Serve garnished with fresh chives. Bon appétit!

81. HALIBUT STEAK IN OLIVE-TOMATO SAUCE

 4 Servings

 Ready in about 15 minutes

PER SERVING:
322 Calories; 20.4g Fat; 24.9g Carbs; 10.5g Protein; 5.7g Sugars

Fish steak is one of the easiest things that you can cook in your electric pressure cooker. You can have amazing tastes of fish that used to take about an hour in the oven, but you can pressure cook it in less than 15 minutes. It's up to you! In addition to saving you time, you get a healthier meal.

INGREDIENTS

- 3/4 pound halibut steak, thawed
- 1 teaspoon sea salt
- 1/4 teaspoon ground black pepper
- 1 teaspoon smoked paprika
- 2 tablespoons pickled capers
- 1 (14-ounce) can diced tomatoes
- 2 bell peppers, deveined and chopped
- 2 sprigs fresh flat-leaf parsley
- 1 teaspoon fresh or dried oregano, minced
- 1 cup black salt-cured olives
- 1 tablespoon crushed garlic
- 2 tablespoons extra-virgin olive oil
- 1 tablespoon fresh ground coriander, to serve

COOKING STEPS

1. Prepare the base of your cooker with 1 ½ water and a trivet.

2. Season the halibut steak with salt, pepper, and paprika; add capers and transfer to a heatproof dish.

3. Then, add tomatoes and gently stir to combine; add the pepper, parsley, and oregano; scatter olives and crushed garlic over everything; drizzle everything with olive oil.

4. Insert the dish into the pressure cooker; close and lock the lid. Set the machine to cook at HIGH pressure for 7 minutes. Open the cooker with the quick release method.

5. Nestle the fish into the sauce and serve warm, garnished with fresh coriander.

82. SPICY ANDOUILLE AND MUSSEL CHOWDER

 6 Servings

 Ready in about 20 minutes

PER SERVING: 316 Calories; 18.2g Fat; 18.3g Carbs; 16.1g Protein; 2.5g Sugars

Make this famous mussel chowder in your Instant Pot and provide your family with a healthy meal. Pressure cooking is one of the best ways to cook seafood with vegetables since the shorter cooking time retains the vitamins and maximizes the nutritional value of the vegetables.

INGREDIENTS

- 1 tablespoon olive oil
- 3/4 cup andouille sausage, thinly sliced
- 1 red bell pepper, chopped
- 2 tablespoons minced pickled jalapeño rings
- 1 leek, finely chopped
- 2 cloves garlic, peeled and pressed
- 1 (12-ounce) bottle amber beer
- 1 ½ cups fish broth
- 1/3 teaspoon sea salt flakes
- 1/3 teaspoon garlic pepper
- 1/2 teaspoon sweet Hungarian paprika
- 1/4 cup red wine vinegar
- 1 carrot, trimmed and chopped
- 1 celery stalk with leaves, cleaned and chopped
- 1 medium-sized Yukon gold potato, peeled and diced
- 1 tablespoon Creole seasoning
- 1 pound mussels, scrubbed and debearded
- 2 cups half-and-half

COOKING STEPS

1. Press the "Sauté" button to heat up your Instant Pot. Then, warm olive oil and cook the sausage until no longer pink. Now, add the peppers, leeks and garlic and cook until tender and aromatic.

2. Pour in the beer and stir with a wooden spoon to deglaze the pot; add fish broth, salt flakes, garlic pepper, Hungarian paprika, wine vinegar, carrot, celery, potato and Creole seasoning.

3. Set the machine's timer to cook for 6 minutes at HIGH pressure. Then, perform the quick-release to bring the pressure back to normal.

4. Stir in the mussels and half-and-half. Simmer on "Sauté" setting for 3 to 4 minutes. Bon appétit!

83. KID-FRIENDLY TUNA SALAD TO-GO

 6 Servings

 Ready in about 20 minutes

PER SERVING:
213 Calories; 8.2g Fat; 22.4g Carbs; 13.4g Protein; 3.8g Sugars

This tuna salad is perfect for sandwiches or snacks. The key to success is to top your salad with delicate and velvety mozzarella. Your kids will be delighted!

INGREDIENTS

- 1 ½ tablespoons butter
- 1/2 cup scallions, finely chopped
- 2 garlic cloves, pressed
- 1 (15-ounce) can petite diced tomatoes
- 1 teaspoon seasoned salt
- 1/4 teaspoon cayenne pepper
- 16 ounces dry egg noodles
- 10 ounces light tuna in water, drained
- 2 cucumbers, thinly sliced
- 2 medium-sized carrots, cleaned and chopped
- 1 cup Kalamata olives, pitted and halved
- Mozzarella cheese, for garnish

COOKING STEPS

1. Click the "Sauté" button and melt the butter; then, cook the scallions, and garlic in the hot butter until fragrant and tender.

2. Add the petite diced tomatoes, salt, cayenne pepper, noodles, and tuna. Then, click the "Soup" button and set the timer for 7 minutes. Turn your Instant Pot off.

3. Lastly, use the quick-release method to bring the pressure back to normal; unlock and open the cooker. Allow the mixture to cool completely.

4. Throw in the cucumbers, carrots, and Kalamata olives; adjust the seasonings and serve topped with Mozzarella cheese. Bon appétit!

84. HADDOCK FILLETS WITH PAPRIKA AND MUSTARD SAUCE

 4 Servings

 Ready in about 15 minutes

PER SERVING:
244 Calories; 7.4g Fat; 1.5g Carbs; 37.9g Protein; 0.0g Sugars

This creamy fish usually takes an hour in the regular oven, but in the Instant Pot, it's ready in a fraction of the time.

INGREDIENTS

- 4 haddock fillets
- 1/2 teaspoon ground black pepper
- 1 teaspoon sea salt
- 4 teaspoons Dijon mustard
- 1 teaspoon hot paprika
- 1/4 cup dry white wine, such as Chardonnay
- 3/4 cup chicken broth
- 4 tablespoons heavy cream
- 1 teaspoon arrowroot

COOKING STEPS

1. Season the fish fillets with black pepper and sea salt; press the "Sauté" button and brown the fillets for 2 minutes on each side. Smear one side of each fish fillet with the mustard and season with hot paprika.

2. Add a steamer to the Instant Pot; line the steamer with parchment paper

3. Lower the fish fillets onto the steamer. Pour the wine and broth into the pot. Lock the lid onto the pot.

4. Set the machine to cook at HIGH pressure for 6 minutes. Afterward, perform the quick-release method to drop the pressure; carefully remove the lid.

5. Now, turn the cooker to "Sauté" mode. Whisk the cream and arrowroot in a small mixing bowl until uniform and creamy. Once the cooking juice is boiling, whisk in the slurry.

6. Continue whisking until it has thickened, about 40 seconds. Spoon the sauce over the fillets.

85. RICH VEGETABLE AND SEAFOOD RISOTTO

 6 Servings

 Ready in about 20 minutes

PER SERVING:
356 Calories; 7.0g Fat; 58.2g Carbs; 12.8g Protein; 5.6g Sugars

Looking for a simple seafood recipe to delight your guests? This recipe is both easy and sophisticated. You can substitute any kind of a medium-grain rice for Arborio rice.

INGREDIENTS

- 2 tablespoons olive oil
- 2 garlic cloves, chopped
- 1 shallot, peeled and diced
- 1 parsnip, chopped
- 1 carrot, chopped
- 1 sweet pepper, chopped
- 1 ¾ cups white Arborio rice
- 1 cup shrimp, peeled, deveined, and roughly chopped
- 1 cup littleneck clams, scrubbed
- 1/4 cup dry sherry
- 3 cups fish stock
- 1 cup bottled clam juice
- Sea salt and cracked black peppercorns
- 1/4 cup loosely packed fresh parsley leaves, chopped

COOKING STEPS

1. Select the "Sauté" program to heat up your Instant Pot. Then, heat the olive oil and sauté the vegetables, stirring occasionally, until they have softened.

2. Next, add the rice, shrimp, and clams; continue sautéing for a further 3 minutes; make sure to stir continuously.

3. Add the dry sherry, fish stock, clam juice, salt, and peppercorns. Set the machine to cook at HIGH pressure for 10 minutes.

4. Afterward, use the natural release method. Unlock and open the cooker. Garnish with fresh parsley and eat warm with sour cream.

86. MAHI-MAHI WITH LIMA BEANS

 4 Servings

 Ready in about 45 minutes

PER SERVING: 269 Calories; 12.0g Fat; 25.1g Carbs; 16.5g Protein; 1.4g Sugars

The mahi-mahi, also known as dolphinfish, is a great source of Vitamins B-5 and B-6, as well as Potassium and Selenium. It is lean fish with a mild taste, so it goes well with salsa, beans, spicy food, etc. Don't forget to add a heaping spoonful of love to this recipe!

INGREDIENTS

- 4 mahi-mahi fillets
- 1 teaspoon sea salt flakes
- 1/2 teaspoon mixed peppercorns, freshly cracked
- 1 teaspoon garlic paste
- 1 tablespoon sweet paprika
- 1/2 cup freshly squeezed lemon juice
- 1 cup lima beans
- 3 cups water
- 2 tablespoons fresh cilantro, roughly chopped
- 1 sprig fresh thyme
- 1 sprig fresh rosemary
- 1/3 teaspoon sea salt
- 1/2 teaspoon ground black pepper
- 1 bay leaf
- Salsa, to serve

COOKING STEPS

1. Soak the lima beans for 6 hours or overnight.

2. Add 1 cup of water and a steamer to your Instant Pot.

3. Rub the fish fillets with salt, peppercorns, garlic paste, and paprika; drizzle with fresh lemon juice. Lay the fillets in the steamer; work in batches. Lock the lid onto the pot.

4. Set the machine to cook at HIGH pressure for 6 minutes. Use the quick-release method.

5. To make the beans, clean the inner pot. Then, drain and rinse the lima beans in a colander; transfer them to the electric pressure cooker.

6. Add 3 cups of water and secure the lid; now, choose the "Bean/Chili" setting; pressure cook for 30 minutes.

7. Once the cooking is over, release the pressure. Carefully remove the lid. Add the other ingredients and seal the lid again; hit the "Soup" button and pressure cook for 1 more minute.

8. Lastly, allow pressure to release on its own. Serve with warm mahi-mahi and salsa of choice. Bon appétit!

87. CLASSIC SEAFOOD LENTIL GUMBO

 8 Servings

 Ready in about 35 minutes

PER SERVING:
183 Calories; 5.8g Fat; 9.0g Carbs; 23.4g Protein; 3.5g Sugars

A hearty gumbo soup ready in 35 minutes! Lentil's mild flavor allows the rich and strong flavors of the seafood to shine.

INGREDIENTS

- 2 tablespoons olive oil
- 1-2 garlic cloves, pressed
- 1 yellow onion, chopped
- 2 cups fish stock
- 1 (14-ounce) can diced tomatoes
- 1 cup French green lentils
- 1 sprig dried thyme, leaves only
- 1 sprig dried rosemary, leaves only
- 1/2 teaspoon chili powder
- 1/2 teaspoon cumin powder
- 1 teaspoon fennel seeds
- 1 tablespoon sage, chopped
- 1 teaspoon sea salt flakes
- 1 ½ pounds shrimp, peeled and deveined
- 1 cup shucked oysters
- 1 cup crabmeat
- 1 tablespoon soy sauce

COOKING STEPS

1. Heat the oil in the Instant pot that is turned to the "Sauté" function. Then, sauté the garlic and onion until they have softened, about 4 minutes.

2. Now, add fish stock, canned tomatoes, and lentils, along with all remaining seasonings. Lock the lid onto the pot.

3. Set the machine to cook at HIGH pressure for 20 minutes. Use the quick-release method.

4. Remove the cooker's lid. Again, choose "Sauté" function. Stir in the shrimp, oysters, crabmeat, and soy sauce; simmer until they become pink. Serve in individual bowls. Bon appétit!

88. Easy Creole Butter Haddock

 4 Servings

 Ready in about 20 minutes

PER SERVING:
208 Calories; 5.7g Fat; 0.1g Carbs; 36.4g Protein; 0.0g Sugars

Are you ready for a light and nutritious protein dinner? Haddock is a powerhouse of proteins, vitamins, and minerals. Serve with German potato salad or oven-roasted cabbage on the side.

INGREDIENTS

- 1 ½ tablespoons butter
- 4 frozen haddock fillets
- 1 tablespoon Creole seasoning blend
- Sea salt flakes and freshly cracked green peppercorns, to your liking
- 2 tablespoons red wine vinegar

COOKING STEPS

1. Begin by preheating your Instant Pot on "Sauté" setting; now, melt the butter. Sprinkle the haddock fillets with seasonings; drizzle with wine vinegar.

2. Now, brown them on both sides for about 4 minutes, flipping once.

3. Pour 1 ½ cup of water into the pressure cooker. Lower the browned fillets onto a steamer rack. Secure the lid and set the machine to cook for 7 minutes at LOW pressure. Lastly, use a normal release. Bon appétit!

89. HOLIDAY SEAFOOD AND CORN STEW

 4 Servings

 Ready in about 20 minutes

PER SERVING:
333 Calories; 21.3g Fat; 13.2g Carbs; 22.2g Protein; 3.4g Sugars

With several layers of flavor, this rich, homemade seafood stew always turns out perfect in an electric pressure cooker. Serve with tortilla chips or cornbread.

INGREDIENTS

- 1 tablespoon unsalted butter
- 4 slices pancetta, diced
- 3 garlic cloves, peeled and minced
- 1 cup scallions, chopped
- 1 carrot, chopped
- 1 parsnip, chopped
- 1 stalk celery with leaves, chopped
- 1/2 cup packed sliced fennel
- 1 teaspoon smoked cayenne pepper
- Kosher salt and freshly ground pepper to taste
- 1/2 teaspoon lemon zest
- 2 bay leaves
- 1 (8-ounce) bottle clam juice
- 2 ½ cups vegetable broth
- 1 tablespoon tomato paste
- 1/2 pound skinless bass, cut into 1-inch pieces
- 1/2 pound medium tail-on shrimp, peeled and deveined
- 1 cup fresh corn kernels
- 2 tablespoons chopped flat-leaf parsley, divided
- 2 cups heavy cream

COOKING STEPS

1. Melt the butter in your cooker that is turned to the "Sauté "mode. Cook pancetta until crisp, about 3 minutes, stirring periodically.

2. Add the vegetables and sauté them until they have softened, for 3 to 4 minutes. Add cayenne pepper, salt, black pepper, lemon zest, and bay leaves; stir for 1 minute or until they are aromatic.

3. Next, add clam juice, vegetable broth, tomato paste, and skinless bass.

4. Lock the lid onto the pot. Set the machine to cook at HIGH pressure for 5 minutes. Use the quick-release method and carefully remove the lid.

5. Again, press the "Sauté" button, add the shrimp, corn, parsley, and cream; let them simmer for approximately 3 minutes or until thoroughly heated. Serve at once.

90. SAUCY COD FILLETS WITH CHERRY TOMATOES

 4 Servings

 Ready in about 15 minutes

PER SERVING:
174 Calories; 6.5g Fat; 27.7g Carbs; 6.2g Protein; 13.9g Sugars

Cod is full of very important nutrients and it's a significant protein powerhouse. Adjust the heat to suit by increasing or decreasing the amount of hot paprika. Serve with Italian white wine such as Pinot Grigio.

INGREDIENTS

- 1 ½ tablespoons extra-virgin olive oil
- 1 cup shallots, chopped
- 3 garlic cloves, minced
- 16 cherry tomatoes, halved
- 4 cod fillets
- 1/2 cup roasted vegetable broth
- 1/2 cup rosé wine
- A small pinch of saffron
- 1 teaspoon hot paprika
- 1 tablespoon tomato ketchup
- Salt and ground black pepper, to taste

COOKING STEPS

1. Preheat your cooker by selecting the "Sauté" program.

2. Once hot, warm the oil, and sauté the shallots until just tender; add the garlic and cook until aromatic, or for about 1 minute.

3. Add cherry tomatoes and continue sautéing for a further 1 minute. Place fish fillets on the top. Mix in the remaining ingredients and secure the cooker's lid.

4. Select the "Manual" setting and cook at LOW pressure for 4 minutes. Once cooking is complete, use a normal release.

VEGAN RECIPES

91

95

98

100

105

91. SPICY GARDEN VEGETABLE SOUP

 6 Servings

 Ready in about 15 minutes

PER SERVING:
220 Calories; 4.6g Fat;
40.3g Carbs; 7.7g Protein;
6.8g Sugars

Hard vegetables like potatoes and parsnip are excellent products for the Instant Pot, as are the tougher greens such as cabbage and mustard greens. You don't have to follow a vegan diet to enjoy this thick and spicy vegan soup.

INGREDIENTS

- 1 ½ tablespoons olive oil
- 1 shallot, peeled and finely chopped
- 4 cloves of garlic, minced
- 4 Yukon Gold potatoes, peeled and diced
- 2 large-sized carrots, chopped
- 1 parsnip, chopped
- 1 cup white cabbage, chopped
- 1 sweet bell pepper, deveined and chopped
- 1 chili pepper, deveined and chopped
- 1/3 teaspoon sweet Hungarian paprika
- Himalayan pink salt and freshly cracked mixed peppercorns, to taste
- 3 cups vegetable broth, preferably homemade
- 1/2 cup water
- 1 bunch mustard greens, cleaned and chopped
- 2 tablespoons cider vinegar
- 1 ½ tablespoons all-purpose flour + 2 tablespoons water

COOKING STEPS

1. Hit the "Sauté" key to preheat your Instant Pot. Now, heat olive oil and sauté the shallot until it begins to soften. Now, stir in the garlic and cook until aromatic.

2. You can add broth, one spoon at a time, to prevent food from sticking to the bottom.

3. Next step, add the potatoes, carrots, parsnip, cabbage, and both peppers; season with paprika, salt, and peppercorns. Pour in the remaining broth and water.

4. Close and lock the cooker's lid. Set your machine to cook for 3 minutes at HIGH pressure. After that, allow the pressure to come down naturally. Uncover the pot and puree the vegetables using an immersion blender.

5. Make the slurry by whisking the flour and cold water. Turn the cooker to "Sauté" mode and add the slurry along with mustard greens and cider vinegar; simmer, uncovered, until the cooking liquid has thickened.

92. TURNIP AND PEA STEW

 4 Servings

 Ready in about 25 minutes

PER SERVING:
131 Calories; 4.2g Fat; 20.8g Carbs; 4.9g Protein; 11.3g Sugars

With lots of fresh and tasty vegetables, this savory stew may become a family favorite. If your stew is too watery, you can add cornstarch slurry.

INGREDIENTS

- 1 tablespoon olive oil
- 2 red onions, peeled and chopped
- 2 cloves garlic, minced
- 1 turnip, cut into chunks
- 1 celery stalk with leaves, cleaned and chopped
- 1 large-sized carrot, trimmed and chopped
- 1 sprig rosemary, chopped
- 1 sprig thyme, chopped
- 1 cup peas
- 1 cup water
- 1 cup vegetable stock
- 4 ripe plum tomatoes, seeded and chopped
- 2 tablespoons dry rosé wine
- Sea salt and freshly ground black pepper, to savor

COOKING STEPS

1. Press the "Sauté" button on your cooker and heat the oil. Now, sauté the onions and garlic until tender and aromatic.

2. Stir in the turnip, celery, carrot, rosemary, and thyme; sauté for a further 2 minutes. Stir in the peas, water and vegetable stock.

3. Choose the "Manual" setting and pressure cook for 15 minutes. Press the "Cancel" button and release pressure naturally.

4. Program it back to "Sauté" mode. Now, stir in tomatoes, wine, salt, and black pepper. Simmer for 4 minutes, stirring often. Bon appétit!

93. AROMATIC BASMATI RICE WITH ROASTED PEANUTS

 6 Servings

 Ready in about 30 minutes

PER SERVING:
407 Calories; 26.9g Fat; 38.7g Carbs; 17.7g Protein; 7.1g Sugars

Basmati rice has short cooking time and fine texture, which makes it a perfect side dish. If you could add a vegan cheese over the top, it would be a delightful main course.

INGREDIENTS

- 1 ½ tablespoons peanut oil
- 1 cup scallions, chopped
- 1 teaspoon dried basil
- 1/4 teaspoon turmeric powder
- 1 teaspoon granulated garlic
- 1 ripe Roma tomato, seeded and chopped
- 1 ¾ cups basmati rice
- 2 ¾ cups vegetable broth
- Salt and pepper, to taste
- A dash of ground allspice
- 1 cup roasted peanuts, to serve

COOKING STEPS

1. Begin by preheating your cooker on "Sauté" mode. Now, warm the peanut oil and sauté the scallions for approximately 4 minutes or until they have softened.

2. Add dried basil, marjoram, turmeric, garlic, and chopped tomato; continue sautéing for about 2 minutes.

3. Stir in basmati rice and cook for 1 to 2 minutes more. Now, pour in the broth; season with salt, pepper, and allspice and stir to combine well.

4. Secure the lid according to the manual. Set the machine to cook at HIGH pressure for 13 minutes. Allow the pressure to release on its own.

5. Finally, fluff the rice with a wooden spoon and serve topped with roasted peanuts. Enjoy!

94. RUSTIC POTATO AND ROASTED PEPPER SOUP

 4 Servings

 Ready in about 20 minutes

PER SERVING:
198 Calories; 5.5g Fat; 34.1g Carbs; 5.3g Protein; 5.5g Sugars

Vegan diet and pressure cooking go hand in hand. This rustic and tasty combination of vegetables proves that. Just follow these simple steps, sit down and enjoy a bowl of the flavorful soup.

INGREDIENTS

- 1 ½ tablespoons olive oil
- 1 shallot, chopped
- 3 garlic cloves, peeled and pressed
- 1 bay leaf
- 1 celery stalk, chopped
- 1 celery rib, chopped
- 1 carrot, trimmed and chopped
- 1/2 cup diced roasted red bell peppers
- 2 russet potatoes, peeled and cubed
- 5 cups vegetables stock
- 1 bunch kale, thick middle ribs removed, torn into pieces
- Salt and pepper, to taste

COOKING STEPS

1. Hit the "Sauté" button and heat olive oil; then, sauté the shallot until it begins to soften; now, add the garlic and bay leaf, and continue sautéing until aromatic and just browned.

2. Add the remaining ingredients and set your machine to cook for 9 minutes at HIGH pressure. Open the cooker with the quick release method.

3. Using an immersion hand blender, puree the mixture until your desired consistency is reached. Serve warm with French bread.

95. SPRING RISOTTO WITH SPINACH AND WALNUTS

 6 Servings

 Ready in about 35 minutes

PER SERVING:
262 Calories; 6.9g Fat; 42.4g Carbs; 7.5g Protein; 1.1g Sugars

This is an incredibly versatile dish; you can experiment with herbs and dress up your plate according to your personal preferences. Enjoy!

INGREDIENTS

- 1 tablespoon dairy-free soy margarine
- 2 tablespoons green garlic, minced
- 1 cup spring onion, chopped
- 1 ½ cups Arborio rice
- 4 cups vegetable stock
- 2 tablespoons dry white wine
- Kosher salt and black pepper, to taste
- 1 teaspoon red pepper flakes, crushed
- 1/2 teaspoon fresh mint leaves, chopped
- 1 tablespoon fresh cilantro
- 2 cups chopped spinach
- 1/3 cup walnuts, toasted and finely chopped
- 2 tablespoons nutritional yeast

COOKING STEPS

1. Heat up your cooker on the "Sauté" setting and warm the margarine; then, cook the garlic and onions until they start to glisten.

2. Stir in Arborio rice, adding the stock, one tablespoon at a time, as needed; cook for 1 to 2 minutes.

3. Now, add the stock, wine, salt, black pepper, and red pepper flakes. Secure the cooker's lid; choose "Rice" function and cook for 25 minutes at HIGH pressure.

4. Once cooking is complete, allow the pressure to come down on its own. Carefully open the cooker and add the spinach. Program it back to "Sauté" mode and cook until the spinach is completely wilted.

5. Afterward, add toasted walnuts and nutritional yeast, give it a good stir and serve in individual bowls.

96. VEGAN APPLE PIE OATMEAL

 4 Servings Ready in about 30 minutes

PER SERVING:
202 Calories; 8.7g Fat; 26.2g Carbs; 5.2g Protein; 13.3g Sugars

This is a perfect meal for an autumn morning. It is like a dessert for breakfast to uplift your mood at the beginning of the day!

INGREDIENTS

- 2 tablespoons vegan margarine
- 3/4 cup steel cut oats
- 1 ½ cups coconut milk
- 1 ½ cups water
- 1 apple, cored, peeled, and diced
- A pinch of salt
- 1 tablespoon maple syrup
- 1 teaspoon coconut extract
- 1/2 teaspoon almond extract
- 1 teaspoon apple pie spice mix
- A pinch of grated nutmeg

COOKING STEPS

1. To preheat the Instant Pot, select "Sauté" mode. Once hot, melt the margarine and then, cook the oats for 1 to 2 minutes, stirring frequently.

2. Stir in the other ingredients, minus grated nutmeg. Secure the lid. Then, choose the "Manual" key and cook at HIGH pressure for 8 minutes.

3. Afterward, allow pressure to drop naturally for 10 minutes, then, release any remaining steam. Serve with a few sprinkles of grated nutmeg and some extra slices of apples. Bon appétit!

97. Curry Coconut Sweet Potato-Apple Soup

 6 Servings

 Ready in about 30 minutes

PER SERVING:
258 Calories; 14.0g Fat; 33.1g Carbs; 3.1g Protein; 9.4g Sugars

Your family will love spending their fall afternoon dipping crackers into this velvety creamy soup. Don't forget to add a pinch of your favorite seasonal spices to make your recipe outstanding!

INGREDIENTS

- 1 tablespoon coconut oil
- 1 yellow onion, peeled and finely chopped
- 2 cloves garlic minced
- 4 sweet potatoes, peeled and cubed
- 1 tart apple, cored, peeled and diced
- 3 carrots, trimmed and diced
- 1/2 teaspoon cinnamon
- A pinch of nutmeg
- A pinch of kosher salt
- 1 tablespoon yellow curry powder
- 1/4 teaspoon grated fresh ginger
- 1/2 teaspoon rubbed sage
- 3 cups vegetable stock
- Salt, to taste
- 2 ounces applesauce, unsweetened
- 10 ounces light coconut milk

COOKING STEPS

1. Heat up your Instant Pot on "Sauté" mode and warm the coconut oil. Then, sweat the onions until they start to glisten; add the garlic and sauté until just tender and aromatic.

2. Add the remaining ingredients, minus the coconut milk. Close and lock the cooker's lid.

3. Choose the "Manual" setting and cook for 18 minutes at HIGH pressure. After that, perform a quick release. Add the coconut milk and click the "Sauté" button; simmer for about 5 minutes, until heated through.

4. Puree the soup to your desired consistency using an immersion hand blender. Serve with crackers. Bon appétit!

98. Cranberry Pear Breakfast Risotto

 4 Servings

 Ready in about 15 minutes

PER SERVING: 280 Calories; 14.4g Fat; 36.9g Carbs; 3.0g Protein; 14.9g Sugars

What's more comforting than a bowl of fruit risotto on a cold morning? Pressure cook fine, buttery jasmine rice in less than 15 minutes, add fruits and enjoy!

INGREDIENTS

- 2 cups coconut milk
- 1/2 cup pear cider
- 1 cinnamon stick
- 3-4 whole cloves
- 1/4 teaspoon freshly grated nutmeg
- A pinch of table salt
- 1/2 cup jasmine rice
- 3 orange zest strips
- 3 tablespoons agave nectar
- 1/2 cup dried cranberries
- 1 pear, cored and chopped

COOKING STEPS

1. Heat up your cooker by selecting the "Sauté" button. Once hot, pour in coconut milk and bring to a gentle boil.

2. Then, stir in the cinnamon stick, cloves, nutmeg, salt, rice, orange zest strips, agave nectar, and pear cider; give it a good stir.

3. Secure the cooker's lid. Select the "Manual" setting and cook for 5 minutes at HIGH pressure.

4. Once cooking is complete, select the "Cancel" button and release the pressure naturally. Use a fork to fluff up your rice. Fold in dried cranberries and pears. Bon appétit!

99. EASIEST MEDITERRANEAN BAKED POTATOES EVER

 6 Servings

 Ready in about 20 minutes

PER SERVING:
209 Calories; 0.3g Fat; 47.5g Carbs; 5.1g Protein; 3.5g Sugars

Extra-virgin olive oil and a few sprinkles of aromatic Mediterranean herbs will bring back memories of the summer, while olives such as Beldi will add salty depth to your potatoes. All these ingredients turn simple baked potatoes into a decadent dish.

INGREDIENTS

- 4 pounds russet potatoes, peeled and quartered
- 1 sprig rosemary
- 1 sprig thyme
- 1 teaspoon sea salt
- Freshly cracked mixed peppercorns
- 2 tablespoons extra-virgin olive oil
- Black olives, to serve

COOKING STEPS

1. Prepare your Instant Pot by adding a steamer and 1 cup of water. Place the potatoes in the steamer.

2. Close and lock the cooker's lid. Then, set your machine to cook for 7 minutes at HIGH pressure.

3. After that, allow the pressure to come down naturally. Toss the potatoes with seasonings and EVOO. Serve immediately with black olives.

100. VIDALIA AND SWEET POTATOES WITH DIJON SAUCE

 4 Servings

 Ready in about 25 minutes

PER SERVING: 285 Calories; 13.6g Fat; 38.9g Carbs; 3.1g Protein; 2.1g Sugars

Easy, fun and healthy... What more could we want from our meal? These fluffy, baked short-cut sweet potatoes are served with tangy, sweet mustard sauce. Lovely!

INGREDIENTS

- 4 medium-sized sweet potatoes, peeled
- 1 Vidalia onion, peeled and sliced
- 1 teaspoon dried thyme
- 1 teaspoon dried sage
- Salt and pepper, to taste
- 1 ½ tablespoons olive oil

For Dijon Sauce:

- 2 ½ tablespoons cashew butter
- 3/4 tablespoon Dijon mustard
- 2 ½ tablespoons agave nectar
- 1/4 teaspoon seasoned salt
- 1/2 teaspoon paprika
- 1 tablespoon dry white wine

COOKING STEPS

1. Place the sweet potatoes on aluminum foil. Pierce them with a fork and top with the slices of Vidalia onions.

2. Now, sprinkle with dried thyme, sage, salt, and pepper; drizzle with olive oil. Finally, wrap the potatoes in foil.

3. Prepare the pot by adding a trivet and about 1 cup of water to the bottom. Secure the lid and set your machine to cook at HIGH pressure for 15 minutes.

4. Meanwhile, prepare the Dijon sauce by mixing all of the sauce ingredients; whisk well and set aside.

5. When pressure cooking is done, open the cooker by releasing the pressure. Use a natural release. Serve on individual plates with Dijon sauce. Bon appétit!

101. STEAMED GREEN BEANS IN GARLIC SAUCE

 4 Servings

 Ready in about 15 minutes

PER SERVING:
142 Calories; 7.7g Fat; 17.6g Carbs; 2.0g Protein; 2.2g Sugars

Green beans are high in fiber and nutrients. Serve them with this easy garlic sauce for a guilt-free dinner. Enjoy!

INGREDIENTS

- 2 ½ cups frozen green beans
- 1 teaspoon garlic salt
- 1/2 teaspoon red pepper flakes, crushed
- 2 tablespoons sesame oil
- 4 garlic cloves, peeled and pressed
- 1/2 cup scallions
- Salt and pepper, to your liking
- A dash of ground allspice
- 1 tablespoon Worcestershire sauce
- 1 ½ cups rice milk
- 1 tablespoon lime juice

COOKING STEPS

1. Add 1 to 1 ½ cups of water to the Instant Pot; now, place a steamer basket on top. Add green beans and secure the lid.

2. Select "Steam" and cook at HIGH pressure for 3 minutes. Season with salt and red pepper flakes.

3. In the meantime, make the sauce. In a saucepan, heat the oil over a moderate flame; cook the garlic and scallions until just tender.

4. Transfer to your blender along with the other ingredients; puree until uniform and smooth.

5. Serve with steamed green beans. Bon appétit!

102. MOM'S SAUCY PASTA WITH CAULIFLOWER

 4 Servings

 Ready in about 20 minutes

PER SERVING: 432 Calories; 8.2g Fat; 75.3g Carbs; 15.4g Protein; 7.1g Sugars

You can change out these seasonings based on your preference using the other herb mix. However, Italian herb mix is a nice and useful addition to any well-stocked kitchen!

INGREDIENTS

- 1 ½ tablespoons peanut oil
- 1 cup leeks, chopped
- 2 cloves garlic, peeled and pressed
- 1 carrot, cleaned chopped
- 1 cup cauliflower florets
- 1/2 teaspoon yellow mustard
- 1 tablespoon Italian herb mix
- Salt and pepper, to your liking
- 1 ½ cups homemade roasted vegetable stock
- 1 ½ cups water
- 2 plum tomatoes, seeded and chopped
- 1 red bell pepper, deveined and chopped
- 1 chipotle pepper, deveined and chopped
- Salt and pepper, to taste
- 1 teaspoon paprika
- 1/2 teaspoon ground bay leaves
- 1 teaspoon porcini powder
- 1 ½ tablespoons Shoyu sauce
- 16 ounces elbow pasta

COOKING STEPS

1. Start by preheating your Instant Pot using the "Sauté" function. Once hot, heat peanut oil and sweat the leeks and garlic until aromatic.

2. Then, add the carrot and cauliflower florets, along with yellow mustard, Italian herb mix, salt and pepper; cook until just tender, stirring periodically.

3. Now, add a splash of homemade stock to scrape off all the crusty brown bits stuck to the bottom of your cooker.

4. Add the other ingredients and set your Instant Pot to cook for 5 minutes at HIGH pressure. Check the pasta for doneness; if it's not cooked enough, push the "Sauté" button and cook with the top off until done.

5. Afterward, perform the quick release option. Serve warm and enjoy!

103. ALL-IN-ONE POT SUMMER CABBAGE

 4 Servings

 Ready in about 15 minutes

PER SERVING:
208 Calories; 6.0g Fat; 29.7g Carbs; 5.3g Protein; 12.8g Sugars

Cabbage always turns out well in a pressure cooker. Keep in mind that you can replace the wine with vegetable stock; if so, add a tablespoon of wine vinegar.

INGREDIENTS

- 1 ½ tablespoons olive oil
- 1 cup yellow onions, peeled and chopped
- 2 garlic cloves, chopped
- 1 large-sized head of white cabbage, cut into strips
- 1 large-sized carrot, chopped
- 1 large red bell pepper, deveined and chopped
- 1/3 cup dry white wine
- 1 bay leaf
- 2 fresh thyme sprigs
- 2 tablespoons rosemary sprig
- 1 ½ cups vegetable stock
- Salt and ground black pepper, to taste
- 1 tablespoon nutritional yeast
- 1 ½ tablespoons cornstarch dissolved in 2 tablespoons water

COOKING STEPS

1. Start by preheating your Instant Pot on the "Sauté" setting. Once hot, warm the oil and sweat the onion and garlic until just tender.

2. Now, add the remaining ingredients, minus the cornstarch slurry; give it a good stir.

3. Then, choose "Manual" mode and cook for 9 minutes at HIGH pressure. Once cooking is complete, perform a quick release. Make sure to release any remaining stem before removing the cooker's lid.

4. Program it back to "Sauté" mode and add the slurry; let it simmer for a few more minutes or until cooking juice has thickened.

104. FAVORITE WHEAT BERRIES WITH SAUTÉED VEGETABLES

 6 Servings

 Ready in about 40 minutes

PER SERVING:
161 Calories; 4.6g Fat; 25.7g Carbs; 5.7g Protein; 5.8g Sugars

According to Wikipedia, "A wheat berry or wheatberry is an entire wheat kernel (except for the hull), composed of the bran, germ, and endosperm." Wheat berries are packed with protein and fiber, along with B Vitamins.

INGREDIENTS

- 1 ½ tablespoons vegetable oil
- 1 cup scallions, chopped
- 2 garlic cloves, finely minced
- 2 celery stalks with leaves, chopped
- 2 large-sized carrots, cleaned and chopped
- 1 red bell pepper, deveined and chopped
- 1 green bell pepper, deveined and chopped
- 2 tablespoons dry white wine
- 1 teaspoon dried basil
- 1/2 teaspoon dried oregano
- Salt and ground black pepper, to your liking
- 2 ½ cups soft white wheat berries
- 5 cups water
- 1 ½ cups vegetable broth
- 1 heaping tablespoon of fresh cilantro, roughly chopped

COOKING STEPS

1. Click the "Sauté" button to heat up your Instant Pot. Then, heat the oil and sauté the scallions and garlic until aromatic.

2. Now, stir in the celery with leaves, carrot, and bell pepper. Add the basil, oregano, salt, pepper; then, continue sautéing for a further 3 minutes or until they begin to soften.

3. Add the wine to deglaze the pot using a wooden spoon; reserve the sautéed mixture.

4. After that, clean the pot; add the soaked wheat berries along with the water and broth into the pot. Allow the pressure to come down on its own and carefully remove the lid. Check your wheat berries for doneness.

5. Next step, add the sautéed mixture, click the "Sauté" button again and simmer for about 15 minutes.

6. Let the mixture cool for 10 to 15 minutes before plating and topping with fresh cilantro. Bon appétit!

105. THAI-STYLE SWEET CORN SOUP

 8 Servings

 Ready in about 25 minutes

PER SERVING: 220 Calories; 10.2g Fat; 31.8g Carbs; 4.9g Protein; 7.2g Sugars

This authentic and lightly spicy soup with bold, irresistible flavors is the perfect starter for a late summer lunch. Your kids will love it as well.

INGREDIENTS

- 1 tablespoon coconut oil
- 1 cup scallions, chopped
- 1 teaspoon garlic paste
- 2 sweet potatoes, peeled and chopped
- 2 carrots, peeled and chopped
- 1 parsnip, chopped
- 4 ears fresh sweet corn, husked
- 1/2 teaspoon mixed peppercorns, freshly cracked
- 1 bay leaf
- 1/2 teaspoon smoked paprika
- Pink Himalayan salt, to your liking
- 4 ½ cups vegetable stock
- 1 tablespoon soy sauce
- 1 tablespoon sherry vinegar
- 1 (14-ounces) can light coconut milk
- Diced red pepper, for garnish

COOKING STEPS

1. Heat up your Instant Pot by using the "Sauté" setting. Melt coconut oil and sauté the scallions until just tender.

2. Now, add garlic paste, along with sweet potatoes, carrots, and parsnip. Sauté the vegetables for approximately 4 minutes, or until they're tender.

3. After that, add sweet corn, peppercorns, bay leaf, paprika, salt, and stock.

4. Set the machine to cook at HIGH pressure for 6 minutes. Allow the pressure to come down on its own. Pour in soy sauce, sherry vinegar and coconut milk and set the cooker to the "Sauté" function.

5. Let it simmer, uncovered, for about 5 minutes or until it is thoroughly warm and slightly thick. Serve with diced red pepper. Bon appétit!

SNACKS & APPETIZERS

117

107

110

113

120

106. CORN WITH COTIJA CHEESE AND HUNGARIAN PAPRIKA

 4 Servings

 Ready in about 15 minutes

PER SERVING: 246 Calories; 11.2g Fat; 29.4g Carbs; 12.0g Protein; 5.2g Sugars

If you don't have a grill, you can pressure cook your corn. This is a great way to serve a healthy snack. Cheesy, spicy and simple, this corn is irresistible.

INGREDIENTS

- 4 ears of corn, broken into halves
- Salt and pepper, to taste
- 1 tablespoon Hungarian paprika
- 1 cup Cotija cheese, grated

COOKING STEPS

1. Prepare your pot by adding 1 cup of water and a steamer rack.

2. Place the corn on the rack; Set your machine to "Manual". Cook for 9 minutes at HIGH pressure.

3. Afterward, perform a quick release. Rub each ear of corn with the remaining ingredients. Transfer to a nice serving platter and serve immediately.

107. GARLICKY SAUTÉED MUSTARD GREENS

 4 Servings

 Ready in about 15 minutes

PER SERVING:
97 Calories; 7.1g Fat; 6.9g Carbs; 3.5g Protein; 2.0g Sugars

This is an effective, delicious appetizer full of valuable nutrients. Serve with sparkling wine as an aperitif. Enjoy!

INGREDIENTS

- 1 pound mustard greens, stems removed, cut into small pieces
- 2 tablespoons sesame oil
- 4 cloves garlic, minced
- 1 teaspoon soy sauce
- Salt and black pepper, to taste
- 1/2 cup fresh chopped chives

COOKING STEPS

1. Prepare your Instant Pot by adding the steamer basket and 1 ½ cups of water to the bottom.

2. Add the mustard greens to the steamer basket. Secure the cooker's lid. Use the "Manual" button and set the machine to cook for 7 minutes at HIGH pressure.

3. Afterward, use a quick release and carefully remove the lid. Toss with sesame oil, garlic, soy sauce, salt, pepper, and chives. Bon appétit!

108. PARTY MARINATED CHICKEN THIGHS

 4 Servings

 Ready in about 30 minutes + marinating time

PER SERVING:
263 Calories; 10.8g Fat; 5.3g Carbs; 33.6g Protein; 4.0g Sugars

You'll wow your party guests with these golden and succulent chicken thighs. To serve, use your favorite sauce like teriyaki, buffalo, etc.

INGREDIENTS

- 4 tablespoons soy sauce
- 2 ½ tablespoons brown sugar
- 2 tablespoons dry sherry
- 1 teaspoon turmeric powder
- 1/2 teaspoon onion powder
- 1 teaspoon cumin powder
- 1 teaspoon garlic powder
- Kosher salt and black pepper, to taste
- 1 ½ pounds chicken thighs
- 1 tablespoon olive oil

COOKING STEPS

1. Whisk together the soy sauce, sugar, sherry, and seasonings in a bowl. Nestle the chicken thighs into the marinade and cover with plastic wrap; allow it to stand in your fridge for about 3 hours.

2. Prepare your cooker by adding a trivet and 1 cup of running tap water to the bottom. Lay the marinated thighs on top of the trivet.

3. Secure the lid; set the machine to cook for 5 minutes at HIGH pressure. After that, allow the pressure to come down naturally for about 10 minutes; then, release any remaining steam.

4. In a Dutch oven, heat the oil over moderate heat. Then, add the cooked wings, along with the remaining marinade.

5. Fry for 3 minutes, working in batches. Serve with your favorite wing sauce. Enjoy!

109. LAMB AND FETA COCKTAIL MEATBALLS

 10 Servings

 Ready in about 15 minutes

PER SERVING: 258 Calories; 11.2g Fat; 5.3g Carbs; 32.2g Protein; 1.3g Sugars

Homemade meatballs are always a good idea for any gathering. These bites are also kid-friendly. Whip up the cocktail meatballs and serve with delicate and easy sauce of choice.

INGREDIENTS

- 2 garlic cloves, crushed
- 2 pounds lamb meat ground
- 1/2 pound feta cheese, crumbled
- 1 egg, beaten
- 1/2 cup breadcrumbs
- 2 tablespoons fresh parsley, finely chopped
- 1 tablespoon fresh mint, finely chopped
- 1/2 teaspoon kosher salt, plus more for sauce
- 1/4 teaspoon freshly ground black pepper
- 1 tablespoon Worcester sauce

COOKING STEPS

1. In a large mixing bowl, combine the garlic, lamb, feta, egg, breadcrumbs, parsley, mint, salt, pepper, and Worcester sauce. Form the mixture into 1-inch balls and place them in the freezer; allow them to harden for a few hours.

2. Add 1 cup of water and a steamer basket to the bottom of your cooker. Lower the frozen meatballs onto the steamer basket. Secure the lid. Set your machine to pressure cook for 5 minutes under HIGH pressure.

3. Allow the pressure to release naturally and carefully remove the cover. Transfer the cooked meatballs to a nice serving platter. Serve with cocktail picks and your favorite sauce.

110. RICH POTATO APPETIZER SALAD

 6 Servings

 Ready in about 25 minutes

PER SERVING: 310 Calories; 10.9g Fat; 51.0g Carbs; 11.4g Protein; 3.3g Sugars

Pressure cooker transforms a regular potato salad into a festive rich appetizer! If your mouth is already watering, give this recipe a try!

INGREDIENTS

- 8 Yukon gold potatoes, peeled and diced
- 1½ tablespoons extra-virgin olive oil
- 1 teaspoon dried rosemary
- Salt, to taste
- 4 slices bacon, chopped
- 1 shallot, chopped
- 3 garlic cloves, peeled and crushed
- 2 tablespoons wine vinegar
- 1/2 teaspoon ground mixed peppercorns
- 1 teaspoon bay leaf powder
- 1/3 teaspoon cumin powder

COOKING STEPS

1. Prepare your cooker by adding 1 ½ cups of water and a steamer basket to the bottom. Now, lay the potatoes in the steamer basket. Set the machine to cook for 5 minutes under HIGH pressure.

2. After that, perform a quick pressure release; now, remove the lid according to the manufacturer's instructions. Add the potatoes along with olive oil, rosemary, and salt to taste. Place in the refrigerator until the serving time.

3. In the meantime, fry the bacon and shallot in a nonstick skillet over a moderate flame, about 7 minutes. Reserve.

4. Remove from the heat and add the remaining ingredients; stir to combine well. Spoon over chilled potatoes and serve with some extra chopped shallots if desired.

111. MAPLE AND SAGE CARROT STICKS

 8 Servings

 Ready in about 15 minutes

PER SERVING:
88 Calories; 1.5g Fat;
18.3g Carbs; 1.3g Protein;
11.6g Sugars

This delicious snack is low in cholesterol and high in dietary fiber, potassium and Vitamin A. It's a great way to avoid unhealthy proceed food and serve good-for-you, afternoon energy boosters!

INGREDIENTS

- 2 pounds Dutch carrots, peeled and cut into thick sticks
- 3/4 tablespoon butter, at room temperature
- 1/4 cup maple syrup
- 1/4 teaspoon paprika
- 1 tablespoon wholegrain mustard
- Kosher salt and ground black pepper, to taste
- Fresh sage leaves, to serve

COOKING STEPS

1. Prepare the cooker by adding 1 cup of water to the pot; place a steamer basket on top. Lay the carrot sticks in the steamer basket and secure the cooker's lid according to the manual.

2. Select the "Steam" function and cook at HIGH pressure for 2 minutes. Once cooking is complete, perform a quick release. Carefully remove the steamer basket using the tongs.

3. Next, completely dry the pot before preheating your cooker on "Sauté" mode; warm the butter. Once the butter has melted, add the carrots, along with the other ingredients, minus sage.

4. Stir well until the carrot sticks are fully coated; serve immediately garnished with fresh sage leaves. Bon appétit!

112. CRISPY HERBY SWEET POTATO BALLS

 10 Servings

 Ready in about 1 hour

PER SERVING:
212 Calories; 4.7g Fat; 38.4g Carbs; 4.5g Protein; 1.3g Sugars

Why settle for regular sweet potatoes when you can have crispy, golden sweet potato puffs? Quick pressure cooking also ensures that sweet potatoes retain their valuable nutrients.

INGREDIENTS

- 2 ½ pounds sweet potatoes, peeled and diced
- 2 tablespoons minced scallions
- 1/2 teaspoon mixed peppercorns, freshly cracked
- 3/4 teaspoon sea salt flakes
- 1 teaspoon dried rosemary
- 1/2 teaspoon dried marjoram
- 1/4 teaspoon pumpkin pie spice
- 1 teaspoon garlic powder
- 1/2 teaspoon shallot powder
- 1 ½ tablespoons butter
- 3 tablespoons goat cheese
- 1 egg, beaten
- 3/4 cup breadcrumbs
- 4 tablespoons almond meal

COOKING STEPS

1. Add 1 ½ cups of water and a trivet to the Instant Pot. Place the sweet potatoes on the trivet. Set your machine to cook for 8 minutes under HIGH pressure.

2. Once cooking is complete, perform a quick release; uncover and carefully remove the trivet and water.

3. Mash the sweet potatoes with the minced scallions and all of the seasonings. Add the butter and goat cheese and mash everything together. Let it cool.

4. Refrigerate mashed potatoes for 30 minutes or until chilled. Roll into bite-sized balls.

5. Add a beaten egg to a shallow bowl; place the breadcrumbs and almond meal into another shallow bowl and mix to combine. Dip the potato balls in the beaten egg; then, roll them over the breadcrumb mixture.

6. Lightly grease the balls with a nonstick cooking spray. Bake the sweet potato balls in the preheated oven at 425 degrees F for about 17 minutes. Bon appétit!

113. Orange Glazed Chicken Drumettes

 8 Servings

 Ready in about 25 minutes

PER SERVING:
290 Calories; 6.8g Fat;
4.4g Carbs; 49.6g Protein;
3.1g Sugars

Every home cook has their own secret ingredient to the chicken wings and drumettes. What is your favorite secret recipe ingredient for this amazing appetizer?

INGREDIENTS

- 1 tablespoon butter, at room temperature
- 3/4 wing sauce
- 2 ½ tablespoons hoisin sauce
- 1 teaspoon hot paprika
- Salt and pepper, to taste
- 3 pounds chicken drumettes
- 1 (6-ounce) can orange juice concentrate

COOKING STEPS

1. In an inner pot, thoroughly whisk the butter, wing sauce, hoisin sauce, paprika, salt, and pepper. Nestle the drumettes into the sauce.

2. Then, choose "Manual" mode and cook for 10 minutes under HIGH pressure. Allow the pressure to drop naturally and carefully remove the lid.

3. In the meantime, set your oven to "Broil". Arrange the cooked chicken drumettes on a parchment lined baking sheet. Pour orange juice concentrate and the remaining sauce over them.

4. Bake for 1 to 2 minutes or until crisp. Serve with some extra sauce and enjoy!

114. NUTTY AND YUMMY BEET APPETIZER

 6 Servings

 Ready in about 25 minutes

PER SERVING:
124 Calories; 6.0g Fat;
16.6g Carbs; 3.0g Protein;
13.1g Sugars

There are so many reasons to eat more beets; they lower blood pressure, fight inflammation, help improve energy levels, etc. And they are super yummy when cooked in the Instant Pot.

INGREDIENTS

- 2 cups water
- 2 pounds beets, cut into halves
- 2 tablespoons balsamic vinegar
- 1 teaspoon honey
- 1/2 teaspoon kosher salt
- 1/4 teaspoon freshly ground black pepper
- 2 tablespoons olive oil
- 1/2 teaspoon cumin powder
- 2 tablespoons almonds, slivered

COOKING STEPS

1. Pour the water into the Instant Pot. Place the beets on a steamer rack. Close cooker's lid securely.

2. Choose the "Manual" setting and pressure cook for 15 minutes. Allow the pressure to come down naturally. Uncover, drain and rinse the beets.

3. Now, rub off the skins and cut the beets into slices. Transfer them to a salad bowl.

4. In a bowl, combine the vinegar, honey, salt, black pepper, olive oil, and cumin. Drizzle the prepared vinaigrette over the beets and toss to coat.

5. Scatter slivered almonds over everything and serve chilled.

115. BUTTERY MARJORAM FINGERLING POTATOES

 6 Servings

 Ready in about 30 minutes

PER SERVING:
172 Calories; 7.1g Fat; 24.6g Carbs; 3.6g Protein; 1.6g Sugars

Small baby potatoes in a buttery sauce with herbs. Sounds delicious! You can serve these potatoes with creamy parmesan sauce for dipping.

INGREDIENTS

- 3 ½ tablespoons butter, melted
- 2 pounds fingerling potatoes
- 2 garlic cloves, pressed
- 1 teaspoon dried marjoram
- 1 teaspoon dried dill weed
- 3/4 cup roasted vegetable broth, preferably homemade
- 1/2 teaspoon seasoned salt
- 1/2 teaspoon freshly cracked black peppercorns

COOKING STEPS

1. Firstly, press the "Sauté" button in order to preheat the cooker. Then, melt the butter. Once hot, stir in the fingerling potatoes, garlic, marjoram, and dill.

2. Cook the potatoes, moving them around with a wooden spatula, about 10 minutes. Add the broth, salt and black pepper.

3. Next, choose "Manual" mode and cook for an additional 9 minutes at HIGH pressure

4. Allow the pressure to release naturally and carefully remove the lid. Now, adjust the seasonings and serve.

116. ZINGY PARSNIP BITES

 6 Servings

 Ready in about 20 minutes

PER SERVING:
138 Calories; 6.6g Fat; 20.0g Carbs; 1.0g Protein; 8.4g Sugars

Your Instant Pot transforms earthy, fresh parsnips into a crispy fast snack with the outstanding flavor of mustard powder and coriander. Ta-da!

INGREDIENTS

- 2 ½ cups parsnip, trimmed and cleaned
- 2 tablespoons ghee
- 1 ½ tablespoons maple syrup
- 1 teaspoon mustard powder
- 1/2 teaspoon ground cumin
- 1/2 teaspoon ground coriander
- Kosher salt and white pepper, to taste

COOKING STEPS

1. Use a peeler or mandolin to cut the parsnips into rounds.

2. Then, heat up the cooker by using the "Sauté" button. Melt the ghee and add the maple syrup, mustard powder, cumin, and parsnip slices; cook until the parsnip is tender.

3. Secure the lid; pressure cook for 10 minutes under HIGH heat.

4. Once cooking is complete, push the "Cancel" key and let it sit for 2 minutes. Then, perform a quick release.

5. Toss the cooked parsnip with ground coriander, salt, and white pepper and serve at room temperature. Bon appétit!

117. ARTICHOKES WITH SPICY MAYONNAISE SAUCE

 6 Servings

 Ready in about 25 minutes

PER SERVING:
93 Calories; 4.4g Fat; 12.6g Carbs; 3.1g Protein; 1.9g Sugars

A flavorful appetizer with a vegetarian flair. Adjust the sauce to suit your taste by increasing or decreasing the seasonings.

INGREDIENTS

- 3 large artichokes
- 5 tablespoons mayonnaise
- 1 teaspoon whole-grain mustard
- 1/2 teaspoon Hungarian paprika
- 3 tablespoons fresh lemon juice
- 1 teaspoon shallot powder
- 1/4 teaspoon porcini powder
- 1 teaspoon granulated garlic
- 1 tablespoon fennel seeds
- Salt and pepper, to taste

COOKING STEPS

1. Firstly, discard the damaged outer leaves of your artichokes. Trim the bottoms to be flat. Remove the tough ends of the leaves; drizzle with fresh lemon juice.

2. Pour 1 ½ cups of water into your cooker; now, insert a steamer basket. Arrange the artichokes in the basket with blooms facing up.

3. Secure the lid. Cook at HIGH pressure for 10 minutes. Once cooking is done, release the pressure naturally. Test your artichokes for doneness and let them cool for 5 minutes.

4. Meanwhile, prepare the sauce by mixing the remaining ingredients; whisk to combine well. Cut the cooked artichokes into halves. Serve warm with the sauce on the side.

118. EGGPLANT AND PEPPER DIPPING SAUCE

 10 Servings

 Ready in about 20 minutes

PER SERVING:
117 Calories; 8.9g Fat; 8.7g Carbs; 2.5g Protein; 4.4g Sugars

Eggplant is a staple in almost every home. It is a powerhouse of many minerals and vitamins. Would you rather have a chunky sauce? If so, don't blend it too much.

INGREDIENTS

- 5 tablespoons olive oil
- 2 ½ pounds eggplant, peeled and diced
- 5 garlic cloves, pressed
- 1 ¼ teaspoons sea salt flakes
- 1 fresh green chili
- 1 cup water
- 1 bell pepper, deveined and minced
- 2 tablespoons chopped fresh mint
- 3 tablespoons lemon juice
- 1 teaspoon ground cumin
- 1/4 teaspoon freshly ground black pepper
- 1/2 cup feta cheese, crumbled
- Hungarian paprika, to serve

COOKING STEPS

1. Heat up your cooker by using the "Sauté" program and warm the oil; once hot, sauté the eggplant pieces for 4 to 6 minutes, moving them around with a wooden spatula. Work in batches.

2. Add the garlic and cook until fragrant. Add the salt, green chili, and water. Secure the lid.

3. Choose "Manual" mode and cook at HIGH pressure for 4 minutes. Once cooking is done, perform a quick release and carefully remove the lid.

4. Add chopped bell pepper and give it a good stir. Add the rest of the above ingredients, minus the paprika; puree with an immersion hand blender until desired consistency is reached.

5. Transfer to a serving bowl and sprinkle with Hungarian paprika. Serve at once with enough pita for dunking. Bon appétit!

119. MUST-SERVE STUFFED EGGS

 10 Servings

 Ready in about 25 minutes

PER SERVING:
110 Calories; 8.3g Fat; 3.3g Carbs; 5.7g Protein; 1.1g Sugars

It's hard to imagine a great cocktail party without stuffed eggs; they never go out of style! Pressure cooking allows you to have easy-to-peel cooked eggs that turn out great every time!

INGREDIENTS

- 10 eggs
- Salt and ground black pepper, to taste
- 1/4 cup fresh chives, minced
- 1/2 cup mayonnaise
- 1 teaspoon balsamic vinegar
- 1/4 cup arugula, finely chopped
- 1 tablespoon fresh basil, finely chopped
- 1 teaspoon Dijon mustard

COOKING STEPS

1. Prepare your cooker by adding 1 cup of water and a steamer rack to the bottom. Lay the eggs on the rack.

2. Secure the cooker's lid and pressure cook for 11 minutes under LOW pressure.

3. When the timer beeps, release the pressure naturally. Carefully remove the lid according to the manual.

4. Peel your eggs and slice them into halves. Then, transfer the yolks to a mixing dish. Now, smash the yolks with a fork and stir in the remaining ingredients; mix to combine well. Taste and adjust the seasonings.

5. Stuff the egg whites with this mayo mixture, arrange the prepared eggs on a serving platter and enjoy!

120. SPICY SAUSAGE AND TOMATO DIP

 10 Servings

 Ready in about 20 minutes

PER SERVING:
111 Calories; 7.9g Fat; 4.9g Carbs; 5.2g Protein; 2.1g Sugars

This sumptuous dipping sauce is so easy to make in the Instant Pot, that it could become a part of your weekly routine. It can make your days more festive!

INGREDIENTS

- 1 tablespoon lard
- 1 shallot, chopped
- 2 cloves garlic, sliced
- 1/2 pound spicy ground sausage
- 1 teaspoon dried basil
- 1 teaspoon dried rosemary
- 1/2 teaspoon dried oregano
- 1/3 teaspoon hot paprika
- 1 sweet pepper, deveined and chopped
- 1 (14.5-ounce) can petite diced tomatoes
- 2 tablespoons flour
- 1/2 teaspoon salt
- 1/2 teaspoon ground black pepper, or to taste
- 1/2 teaspoon cayenne pepper

COOKING STEPS

1. Heat up your cooker by using the "Sauté" button; melt the lard. Then, sauté the shallot and garlic until just tender.

2. Add the sausage and cook until it is browned. Place in the other items.

3. Close and lock the lid according to the manufacturer's instructions; set the timer for 5 minutes and cook at HIGH pressure.

4. Afterward, release the pressure naturally. Serve with veggie sticks. Bon appétit!

BEANS & GRAINS

121. TURKEY CHIPOTLE CHILI WITH SCALLIONS

 8 Servings

 Ready in about 40 minutes

PER SERVING: 407 Calories; 10.1g Fat; 50.5g Carbs; 32.6g Protein; 6.2g Sugars

You probably don't cook chili on a regular basis because it takes so much time. However, if you are lucky enough to use the Instant Pot, it becomes a breeze!

INGREDIENTS

- 1 ½ tablespoons olive oil
- 1 cup scallions, finely chopped
- 2-3 garlic cloves, peeled and minced
- 1 pound ground turkey
- 3 (14-ounce) cans crushed tomatoes
- 1 teaspoon dried basil
- 1/2 teaspoon dried oregano
- 1 teaspoon dried crushed rosemary
- 10 ounces navy beans, soaked, drained and rinsed
- 10 ounces pinto beans, soaked drained and rinsed
- 2 bay leaves
- 1 teaspoon red pepper flakes
- 1/2 tablespoon cumin powder
- A pinch of ground allspice
- 1 teaspoon chipotle powder
- 1 teaspoon hot sauce
- 1 ½ cups water

COOKING STEPS

1. Start by preheating your cooker on "Sauté" mode. Then, heat the oil and sweat the scallions until just fragrant and tender. Now, add the garlic and cook, stirring frequently, until aromatic.

2. Then, add ground turkey, and cook, crumbling with a wooden spatula. After that, add canned tomatoes, basil, oregano, and rosemary. Stir together for 1 to 2 minutes.

3. Add the rest of the above ingredients, minus the hot sauce. Secure the cooker's lid and cook at HIGH pressure for 25 minutes.

4. Afterward, perform a quick release; release any remaining steam and remove the lid. Add hot sauce and stir to combine.

5. Serve in individual bowls garnished with cilantro and cheese-corn toppers.

122. CONGEE WITH SESAME AND VEGETABLES

 6 Servings

 Ready in about 30 minutes

PER SERVING:
329 Calories; 5.1g Fat; 63.2g Carbs; 6.0g Protein; 0.0g Sugars

Congee is a thick, silky and comforting porridge with an Asian flair. Serve for breakfast or lunch with romaine lettuce and sweet corn, but if you prefer a meaty version, just add some extra leftover meat or canned tuna.

INGREDIENTS

- 2 tablespoons toasted sesame oil
- 2 garlic cloves, minced
- 1/2 cup scallions, chopped
- 1 celery stalk with leaves, chopped
- 2 ½ cups congee, rinsed
- 4 cups water
- 1 teaspoon fresh ginger, cut into strips
- Salt and ground black pepper, to taste
- 1/2 teaspoon paprika
- A pinch of allspice
- 1 ½ tablespoons soy sauce
- Toasted sesame seeds, to serve

COOKING STEPS

1. Begin by preheating your Instant Pot on "Sauté" mode. Then, heat sesame oil and sauté the garlic, scallions, and celery until just tender.

2. Stir in the other ingredients, minus the soy sauce and sesame seeds. Choose the "Multigrain" function and cook for 20 minutes at HIGH pressure.

3. Allow the pressure to drop on its own and carefully open the lid. Fluff the cooked congee with a spatula and serve warm garnished with soy sauce and sesame seeds.

123. HOMEMADE PAPRIKA CHEDDAR CORNBREAD

 8 Servings

 Ready in about 25 minutes

PER SERVING:
248 Calories; 11.7g Fat; 29.4g Carbs; 7.2g Protein; 1.8g Sugars

Here's a recipe for homemade cornbread just like your grandma used to make. If you want a simplified version of this recipe, you can purchase a boxed cornbread mix.

INGREDIENTS

- 1 ¼ cups all-purpose flour
- 1 cup yellow cornmeal
- 1/2 cup granulated sugar
- 1 teaspoon baking soda
- 1 tablespoon baking powder
- 1 teaspoon kosher salt
- 1 teaspoon granulated sugar
- 4 tablespoons sunflower oil
- 2 eggs
- 3/4 cup milk
- 1/2 cup cheddar cheese, grated
- 1 teaspoon paprika

COOKING STEPS

1. In a mixing dish, stir together the first seven ingredients; mix until thoroughly combined. Add sunflower oil and mix well. Now add the egg, milk, cheddar cheese, and paprika.

2. Then, spritz the bottom and sides of a baking pan; scrape the batter into the pan.

3. Add 1 cup of water and the trivet to the bottom of your Instant Pot. Lower the baking pan onto the trivet.

4. Secure the lid; bake for 18 minutes under HIGH pressure. Allow the pressure to come down naturally; unlock and open the cooker.

5. Lastly, check your cornbread for doneness using a toothpick and transfer to a cooling rack. Serve warm or at room temperature.

124. Cajun Sausage Oatmeal

 6 Servings

 Ready in about 20 minutes

PER SERVING: 379 Calories; 24.6g Fat; 24.2g Carbs; 15.5g Protein; 2.7g Sugars

Instant Pot turns regular oatmeal into an amazing savory breakfast or brunch. Chicken broth can give the dish a lighter finish; cream of celery soup, a bit heftier.

INGREDIENTS

- 1 ½ tablespoons olive oil
- 1 red onion, peeled and chopped
- 3 cloves garlic, minced
- 10 ounces andouille sausage, sliced into rounds
- 1 ½ cups steel cut oats
- 1 cup vegetable stock
- 2 cups cream of celery soup
- Salt and ground black pepper, to your liking
- 1 teaspoon Cajun seasonings
- 1/2 cup grated yellow cheese

COOKING STEPS

1. Begin by preheating your Instant Pot on "Sauté" mode and add the olive oil. Once hot, cook the onions and garlic until just tender and aromatic.

2. Now, stir in the sausage and cook for a few minutes, until it's brown on all sides. Then, stir in the oats and cook for 1 minute more, scraping the bottom occasionally to loosen browned bits.

3. Add the stock, cream of celery soup, salt, pepper, and Cajun seasonings. Lock the lid onto the pot. Set your machine to cook for 10 minutes at HIGH pressure.

4. Allow the pressure to drop naturally and carefully open the cooker. Fold in grated yellow cheese; stir until fully melted. Bon appétit!

125. Autumn Apple and Walnut Couscous

 6 Servings

 Ready in about 20 minutes

PER SERVING:
343 Calories; 6.7g Fat; 62.0g Carbs; 10.1g Protein; 13.8g Sugars

This rich breakfast can be an impressive kick start to your daily diet, so it's worth finding time to make this recipe. You can substitute pears and even blackberries for apples.

INGREDIENTS

- 2 cups couscous, rinsed
- 4 cups water
- 3 tablespoons granulated sugar
- A pinch of grated nutmeg
- 1/4 teaspoon salt
- 1/2 teaspoon pure almond extract
- 1 teaspoon apple pie spice mix
- 2 apples, cored, and diced
- 1/2 cup walnuts, chopped

COOKING STEPS

1. Simply dump all ingredients, minus apples and walnuts, into your cooker. Lock the lid onto the pot.

2. Set your machine to cook for 8 minutes at HIGH pressure. Use the quick-release method to reduce the pressure to normal. Carefully open the cooker

3. Unlock and open the pot. Stir before serving and divide among individual bowls. Serve topped with apples and chopped walnuts. Bon appétit!

126. HERBED SAUSAGE AND SCALLION GRITS

 4 Servings

 Ready in about 20 minutes

PER SERVING:
239 Calories; 6.2g Fat; 32.7g Carbs; 14.0g Protein; 1.5g Sugars

Chop the scallions and garlic into pieces fine enough to dissolve into the well-seasoned grits, flavoring them subtly in the Instant Pot. For more flavor, use a spicy sausage.

INGREDIENTS

- 1 tablespoon lard
- 3 garlic cloves, minced
- 1 ½ cups scallions
- 1 cup pork sausage, cut into rounds
- 1 teaspoon oyster sauce
- 2 cups chicken stock
- 1 ½ cups boiling water
- 3/4 cup grits
- 2 heaping tablespoons fresh parsley
- 1 teaspoon dried basil
- 1/2 teaspoon dried marjoram
- Salt and black pepper, to taste
- 1 teaspoon red pepper flakes, crushed
- 1 teaspoon porcini powder
- 1 teaspoon fennel seeds
- A pinch of ground allspice
- 1/4 teaspoon hot pepper sauce

COOKING STEPS

1. Preheat your Instant Pot by using the "Sauté" button; add lard. Once hot, sauté the garlic and scallions until just tender. Then, stir in the sausage; cook until no longer pink, moving the pieces around with a wooden spatula.

2. Stir in the remaining ingredients, minus the hot pepper sauce. Secure the lid and select "Manual" mode; cook for 6 minutes at HIGH pressure.

3. Allow the pressure to come down on its own; make sure to release any remaining steam before removing the lid. Serve with hot pepper sauce. Bon appétit!

127. CHEESY TRUFFLED OATMEAL WITH MUSHROOMS

 6 Servings

 Ready in about 30 minutes

PER SERVING:
127 Calories; 7.3g Fat; 12.1g Carbs; 3.8g Protein; 0.0g Sugars

You can substitute extra-virgin olive oil for truffle oil, which has a more pungent flavor. It is cheaper version and you have already added the mushroom in your oatmeal, right?

INGREDIENTS

- 1 ¼ cups steel cut oats
- 2 1/3 cups water
- 1 tablespoon olive oil
- 1 teaspoon minced garlic
- 4 sprigs fresh thyme leaves
- 1 cup button mushrooms, chopped
- Kosher salt and pepper, to taste
- 1 tablespoon black truffle oil
- 1/4 cup Parmesan cheese, grated

COOKING STEPS

1. Prepare your Instant Pot by adding 1 cup of water and a trivet to the bottom. Add the oats and water, along with a pinch of salt, to a heat-proof dish.

2. Secure the lid and choose the "Manual" button. Pressure cook for 7 minutes. Once cooking is complete, perform a quick release.

3. Meanwhile, heat olive oil in a nonstick skillet. Now, sauté the garlic, stirring constantly, for 1 minute or until aromatic.

4. Stir in thyme and mushrooms and cook until the mushrooms release all of the moisture, 5 to 6 minutes. Season with salt and pepper.

5. Divide the cooked oatmeal among six bowls and top them with sautéed mushroom mixture. Drizzle each serving with truffle oil and top with Parmesan cheese. Serve immediately and enjoy!

128. TWO-BEAN EVERYDAY CHILI

 6 Servings

 Ready in about 20 minutes

PER SERVING:
406 Calories; 4.0g Fat; 73.4g Carbs; 23.2g Protein; 11.1g Sugars

INGREDIENTS

- 1 tablespoon olive oil
- 2 large-sized purple onions, chopped
- 4 cloves garlic, peeled and minced
- 1 celery stalk with leaves, chopped
- 1 ½ cups water
- 1 cup roasted vegetable stock, preferably homemade
- 2 carrots, cleaned and chopped
- 1 parsnip, cleaned and chopped
- 2 sweet peppers, deveined and chopped
- 1 chipotle pepper, deveined and chopped
- 1 teaspoon dried basil
- 1 teaspoon cayenne pepper
- 1 teaspoon bay leaf powder
- 1/2 teaspoon onion powder
- 1 teaspoon chili powder
- 1 ½ cups canned Great Northern beans
- 1 ½ cups canned red Kidney beans
- 1 (28-ounce) can petite diced tomatoes
- 1/4 cup fresh cilantro, roughly chopped

Chili is a winter comfort food that is sure to please. Keep in mind that water will make a lighter chili, while homemade vegetable broth will make a richer texture. For even more flavor, top with vegan cheese and jazz up your winter!

COOKING STEPS

1. Push the "Sauté" key. Once hot, add the oil; then, sauté the onion and garlic until just tender and aromatic. After that, stir in the celery and cook until it starts to soften.

2. You can add a few tablespoons of water to prevent burning and sticking. Add the other items, minus canned tomatoes and cilantro. Secure the lid.

3. Select "Manual" function and set your machine to cook at HIGH pressure for 8 minutes. After that, use a normal pressure release.

4. Stir in diced tomatoes and give it a good stir. Serve topped with fresh cilantro. Bon appétit!

129. VEGAN HOLIDAY BLACK-EYED PEAS

 6 Servings

 Ready in about 25 minutes

PER SERVING:
300 Calories; 7.1g Fat; 60.3g Carbs; 28.5g Protein; 5.3g Sugars

This is a vegan version of the classic Southern Black-Eyed Peas. To take your meal over the top, serve with homemade cornbread.

INGREDIENTS

- 1 ½ tablespoons olive oil
- 2 cups leeks, chopped
- 2-3 garlic cloves, minced
- 1 carrot, peeled and diced
- Salt and ground black pepper, to taste
- 2 bay leaves
- 1 teaspoon cayenne pepper
- 1/4 teaspoon cumin powder
- 1/4 teaspoon mustard powder
- 1 teaspoon celery seeds
- 1 pound black-eyed peas, soaked
- 1 cup water
- 3 cups vegetable broth

COOKING STEPS

1. Choose the "Sauté" button to heat up your cooker. Add the oil; once hot, sauté the leeks, garlic, and carrot until just tender.

2. Then, add the remaining ingredients and stir until everything is well incorporated.

3. Next step, select the "Bean/Chili" program; pressure cook for 15 minutes. Once cooking is complete, allow the pressure to come down naturally.

4. Carefully unlock and open the cooker. Serve in individual bowls garnished with fresh chopped chives. Bon appétit!

130. SAUSAGE PILAF WITH HERBS AND ALMONDS

 6 Servings

 Ready in about 1 hour

PER SERVING:
376 Calories; 10.5g Fat; 44.6g Carbs; 24.8g Protein; 3.2g Sugars

If you've never had brown rice pilaf from the Instant Pot, you're missing the fluffiest rice ever! You can substitute pine nuts for almonds, if desired.

INGREDIENTS

- 1 ½ tablespoons olive oil
- 1 carrot, chopped
- 1 parsnip, chopped
- 1 celery stalk, chopped
- 1 celery rib, chopped
- 1 cup green onions, finely chopped
- 3/4 pound pork sausage
- 8 cups chicken broth
- Salt and black pepper, to taste
- 1 ½ cups brown rice, well-rinsed
- 1/2 teaspoon ground turmeric
- 1/4 cup lightly packed fresh dill, finely chopped
- 1/4 cup lightly packed fresh mint, finely chopped
- Slivered almonds, to serve

COOKING STEPS

1. Heat up your cooker by selecting the "Sauté" button. Then, heat the oil and sauté the vegetables until just tender.

2. Stir in the sausage and cook until no longer pink. After that, add the broth, salt, pepper, rice, and ground turmeric. Secure the lid and choose the "Rice" setting.

3. Use the quick-release method to bring the pressure back to normal. Serve topped with fresh dill, mint, and almond slivers. Bon appétit!

131. HERBY POLENTA BOWL WITH PROSCIUTTO

 4 Servings

 Ready in about 20 minutes

PER SERVING:
283 Calories; 8.3g Fat; 42.7g Carbs; 9.0g Protein; 4.3g Sugars

The instant Pot keeps the polenta plump and moist, a good match for the olives and tomatoes. Make sure to purchase a high-quality prosciutto for garnish; it's worth it.

INGREDIENTS

- 2 cups water
- 2 cups vegetable broth
- 2 tablespoons ghee, at room temperature
- 1 ¼ cups polenta
- Kosher salt and pepper, to your liking
- 1 sprig thyme, chopped
- 2 sprigs rosemary, chopped
- 1 teaspoon cayenne pepper
- 4 thin slices of prosciutto, to serve
- 4 tablespoons tomato ketchup, to serve

COOKING STEPS

1. Begin by preheating your Instant Pot; use the "Sauté" function. Add the water, broth, and ghee. Bring it to not quite boil.

2. Now, slowly add the polenta, along with the salt, pepper, thyme, rosemary, and cayenne pepper. Make sure to whisk continuously with a wooden spoon.

3. Then, choose the "Porridge" setting; pressure cook for 8 minutes. Allow the pressure to come down on its own.

4. Remove the lid and divide your polenta among 4 serving bowls; top each bowl with a slice of prosciutto and a tablespoon of ketchup. Eat warm.

Beans & Grains | Instant Pot Cookbook

132. Fancy Mixed Berry Porridge

 6 Servings

 Ready in about 40 minutes

PER SERVING: 266 Calories; 12.0g Fat; 35.8g Carbs; 4.5g Protein; 3.6g Sugars

In this delicious and healthy porridge, mixed berries and seasonings balance each other out, as well as the coconut oil and rice milk. Beyond cozy breakfast, you might want to consider this to be the next brunch with your friends.

INGREDIENTS

- 2 ¼ cups rice milk
- 2 ¼ cups steel cut oats
- 4 tablespoons coconut oil
- 4 cups water
- 2 cups fresh mixed berries
- 1/2 cup agave nectar
- A pinch of salt
- A pinch of grated nutmeg
- 1/2 teaspoon crystallized ginger
- 1/2 teaspoon ground cloves
- 1/2 teaspoon cinnamon powder
- 1/2 teaspoon coconut extract

COOKING STEPS

1. Place all ingredients in the inner pot and stir until everything is well incorporated.

2. Cook for 18 minutes under HIGH pressure. Afterward, perform the quick-release method to return the pot's pressure to normal.

3. Carefully remove the lid and divide the porridge among 6 individual bowls. Bon appétit!

133. KALE, HAM HOCK AND BEAN SOUP

 6 Servings

 Ready in about 55 minutes

PER SERVING:
317 Calories; 2.1g Fat; 55.3g Carbs; 21.9g Protein; 9.0g Sugars

If you love beans and soup, the pressure cooker is a great tool to prepare this all-in-one meal while saving you time and money. You can add chopped smoked ham if desired.

INGREDIENTS

- 1 smoked ham hock
- 2 cups cannellini beans, soaked overnight
- 3/4 cup purple onion, peeled and chopped
- 3 cloves garlic, peeled and minced
- 1 red bell pepper, deveined and chopped
- 1 Serrano pepper, deveined and chopped
- 20 ounces canned crushed tomatoes
- 1 large-sized carrot, cleaned and diced
- 1 parsnip, cleaned and diced
- 1 celery, chopped
- 1 teaspoon porcini powder
- 1 ½ teaspoons sea salt
- 1/2 ground black pepper, to taste
- 1 teaspoon cayenne pepper
- 1 bunch kale

COOKING STEPS

1. Place smoked ham hock and cannellini beans into your cooker; cover with water. Now, lock the lid into place and cook on the "Bean/Chili" function.

2. Allow the pressure to release on its own. Remove the lid and taste the beans for doneness; discard the ham hock.

3. Stir in the other ingredients, minus kale; give it a good stir and lock the lid into place again. Then, select the "Soup" function; pressure cook for 15 minutes.

4. Push the "Cancel" button and use a natural release; make sure to release any remaining pressure. Add the kale and press the "Sauté" button; cook until everything is heated through. Bon appétit!

134. PIZZA-STYLE BAKED BEANS

 10 Servings

 Ready in about 1 hour

PER SERVING: 492 Calories; 11.6g Fat; 71.4g Carbs; 27.8g Protein; 13.5g Sugars

This is not a regular baked beans dish. Those are pizza beans! This recipe has a rich and layered texture thanks to the Italian sausage and mozzarella cheese.

INGREDIENTS

- 2 pounds Great Northern beans, soaked overnight
- 3/4 pound Italian sausage
- 1 cup leeks, chopped
- 4 cloves garlic, minced
- 1 bell pepper, chopped
- 1/2 cup maple syrup
- 2 bay leaves
- 1 (14.5-ounce) can diced tomatoes, drained
- 1 teaspoon dried basil
- 1/2 teaspoon dried basil
- 1/3 teaspoon dried rosemary
- 1 tablespoon cumin powder
- Salt and ground black pepper, to taste
- 1 teaspoon red pepper flakes, crushed
- 1/2 cup grated mozzarella cheese, for garnish

COOKING STEPS

1. Place the beans into the Instant Pot; add enough water to cover the beans completely; use the "Manual" mode to set your cooker; cook at HIGH pressure for 5 minutes. Once the time is over, select the "Cancel" function and use a natural release.

2. Meanwhile, brown the sausage in a cast-iron skillet over a moderate flame. Add the leeks, garlic, and peppers; cook until just tender; transfer to the pot.

3. Add the other ingredients, minus mozzarella; stir to combine. Then, click the "Bean/Chili" button and cook for 40 minutes. Afterward, perform a natural pressure release; carefully remove the cooker's lid.

4. Top with freshly grated mozzarella cheese and serve immediately.

135. HERBY POLENTA SQUARES WITH PARMESAN

 4 Servings

 Ready in about 40 minutes

PER SERVING: 241 Calories; 10.4g Fat; 24.4g Carbs; 11.8g Protein; 0.9g Sugars

Ooey-gooey polenta squares with cheesy goodness! Your family will gobble up these healthy and delicious bites. You can serve them with tomato ketchup if desired.

INGREDIENTS

- 2 cups vegetable broth
- 1 cup water
- 3/4 cup coarse polenta
- Salt and pepper, to taste
- 1/4 teaspoon Five-spice powder
- 1 teaspoon smoked paprika
- 1 teaspoon dried rosemary, crushed
- 1 teaspoon dried basil
- 1/2 teaspoon garlic powder
- 1 cup Parmesan cheese, grated

COOKING STEPS

1. Add the broth, water, polenta, salt, and pepper to the Instant Pot; mix in 1/2 of the seasonings. Stir well and secure the lid according to the manufacturer's instructions.

2. Then, push the "Porridge" button; pressure cook for 6 minutes. Allow the pressure to come down on its own and remove the cooker's lid.

3. Add the remaining seasonings and stir to combine. Spread the mixture on a cookie sheet and refrigerate it for 30 minutes. Cut into squares and serve topped with Parmesan cheese.

DESSERT RECIPES

136

139

141

144

145

136. DATE-VANILLA CIABATTA BREAD PUDDING

 8 Servings   Ready in about 40 minutes

PER SERVING: 298 Calories; 9.1g Fat; 45.3g Carbs; 11.2g Protein; 32.0g Sugars

A 6-inch baking pan or soufflé dish come in handy when making a bread pudding in your Instant Pot. If your dish or steam rack doesn't have handles, create a sling using aluminum foil.

INGREDIENTS

- 4 cups ciabatta bread, cubed into 1-inch squares
- 4 cups milk
- 4 eggs
- 1 tablespoon butter, at room temperature
- A pinch of kosher salt
- 1/3 cup sugar
- 1 tablespoon honey
- 1/2 teaspoon cloves, ground
- 1/4 teaspoon anise star, ground
- 1/4 teaspoon freshly grated nutmeg
- 1 ½ teaspoons vanilla paste
- 1/2 cup dried dates, pitted and chopped

COOKING STEPS

1. Lightly grease an oven-safe dish using a nonstick spray. Put the bread pieces into the dish.

2. In a mixing bowl, beat the milk with eggs and butter. Beat until fully incorporated. Now, add the salt, sugar, honey, cloves, anise, nutmeg, and vanilla. Thoroughly mix to combine.

3. Pour the custard mixture over the ciabatta bread cubes. Submerge the bread cubes in the custard mixture.

4. Slowly fold in the dates and let everything sit for about 10 minutes. Then, add 2 cups of water and a steaming rack to the bottom of your cooker.

5. Then, choose the "Manual" function and set your Instant Pot to cook at HIGH pressure for 20 minutes. Once cooking is complete, use a natural release. Carefully remove the baking dish using a sling or handles. Serve at room temperature.

137. CRANBERRY AND PECAN ZUCCHINI BREAD

 8 Servings

 Ready in about 40 minutes

PER SERVING:
396 Calories; 16.2g Fat; 57.4g Carbs; 6.4g Protein; 26.8g Sugars

Make sure to remove the cooker's lid quickly so that condensation doesn't drip onto your zucchini bread. This zucchini bread tastes great with a topping of whipping cream.

INGREDIENTS

- 1/2 cup canola oil
- 1/2 cup applesauce
- 3 eggs, beaten
- 1 ¾ cups brown sugar
- 1 ¾ cups fresh unpeeled zucchini, grated and thoroughly squeezed
- 3 cups self-rising flour
- 1/2 teaspoon baking powder
- 1/2 teaspoon baking soda
- 1/2 teaspoon espresso powder
- 1 teaspoon pure vanilla essence
- 1/2 teaspoon pure almond extract
- A pinch of kosher salt
- 1/2 teaspoon ground cinnamon
- 1/2 teaspoon ground cloves
- 1 teaspoon ground ginger
- 1/2 cup chopped pecans
- 1/2 cup dried cranberries

COOKING STEPS

1. In a mixing dish, whisk the canola oil, applesauce, eggs and brown sugar.

2. Fold in grated zucchini. Now, add the rest of the above ingredients. Scrape the mixture into a lightly greased soufflé dish.

3. Prepare your Instant Pot by adding 2 cups of water and the metal trivet to the bottom. Place the baking dish on the trivet and seal the cooker's lid.

4. Set the machine to cook for 25 minutes at HIGH pressure. Once cooking is complete, allow the pressure to come down naturally.

5. Carefully remove the cooker's lid and transfer your bread to a cooling rack before slicing and serving. Bon appétit!

138. FESTIVE DRIED FRUIT AND WALNUT PUDDING

 8 Servings

 Ready in about 40 minutes

PER SERVING:
289 Calories; 17.1g Fat;
28.7g Carbs; 4.8g Protein;
14.0g Sugars

Here's a useful trick – leave your Instant Pot closed for additional 5 minutes after the pressure has released completely; otherwise, your pudding will turn dry very quickly. In this recipe, you can substitute currants for Sultanas.

INGREDIENTS

- 1/2 cup dried apricots, chopped
- 1 cup Sultanas
- 1/4 cup orange liqueur
- 1 stick butter
- 1/3 cup fine sugar
- 1 teaspoon vanilla extract
- 1 teaspoon crystallized ginger
- 1/2 teaspoon ground cinnamon
- A pinch of ground cloves
- 2/3 cup crackers, crushed
- 2 eggs
- 3/4 cup cake flour
- 1 teaspoon baking soda
- 1/2 teaspoon baking powder
- A pinch of kosher salt
- 1 ½ cups grated carrots
- 1/3 cup chopped walnuts
- 1/3 cup glacé cherry

COOKING STEPS

1. Firstly, soak the dried apricots and sultanas in the orange liqueur.

2. Then, cream the butter with sugar until fluffy; add the rest of the above ingredients and mix well.

3. Prepare your Instant Pot by adding 1 cup of water to the pot and placing the steam rack on top. Divide the mixture among 8 heat-proof containers.

4. Now, place the containers, side by side, on the rack. Seal the cooker's lid. Cook at HIGH pressure for 15 minutes. After that, perform a quick release.

5. Select the "Manual" button. Set your machine to cook for 40 minutes under LOW pressure. Work in batches.

6. Let the puddings stand until the steam comes down; now, carefully lift them out. Bon appétit!

139. HOLIDAY ORANGE AND RASPBERRY CHEESECAKE

 8 Servings

 Ready in about 40 minutes + chilling time

PER SERVING: Calories; 33.6g Fat; 26.2g Carbs; 8.1g Protein; 14.3g Sugars

This is a first-class cheesecake that tastes like spring and it's ready in no time. Top the chilled cheesecake with the raspberry sauce and enjoy!

INGREDIENTS

- 1 1/3 cups butter cookie crumb
- 3 ½ tablespoons unsalted butter, melted
- 1 ½ tablespoons brown sugar

For the Filling:

- 20 ounces cream cheese, room temperature
- 2/3 cup brown sugar
- 1 ½ tablespoons all-purpose flour
- A pinch of table salt
- 2 tablespoons orange liqueur
- 1/2 teaspoon orange extract
- 3/4 teaspoon vanilla extract
- 2 eggs + 1 egg yolk
- 2 tablespoons grated orange rind

For the Topping:

- 8 ounces frozen raspberries with syrup
- 2 ½ tablespoons caster sugar
- 1/2 teaspoon ground anise star
- 1 teaspoon cornstarch

COOKING STEPS

1. Prepare the Instant Pot by adding 1 ½ cups of water and a steam rack to the bottom. Now, lightly butter the bottom and sides of a springform pan.

2. In a mixing dish, thoroughly combine all of the crust ingredients. Press into the bottom of the pan and almost halfway up the sides.

3. Then, mix the cream cheese and brown sugar until well combined. Stir in the flour, salt, orange liqueur, orange extract, and vanilla extract. Fold in the eggs and grated orange rind; mix until everything is well incorporated. Spread the mixture onto the prepared crust.

4. Place the pan on the steam rack; secure the cooker's lid. Select "Manual" mode and cook at HIGH pressure for 30 minutes. Once cooking is complete, use a natural release. Carefully remove the lid.

5. Let the cheesecake cool to room temperature on a wire rack; then, cover and refrigerate overnight before slicing and serving.

6. Meanwhile, put the raspberries in your refrigerator. Then, puree them, along with syrup, in a food processor.

7. In a saucepan that is preheated over a moderate flame, melt 3 tablespoons of sugar, anise, and cornstarch. Add the raspberry puree. Cook until the sauce has thickened; cool the sauce to room temperature and serve over cheesecake.

140. MAPLE AND FIG YOGURT DESSERT

 8 Servings

 Ready in about 8 hours + chilling time

PER SERVING: 347 Calories; 17.4g Fat; 48.9g Carbs; 5.4g Protein; 37.9g Sugars

A fruit yogurt is always a good idea for an afternoon snack and it's extra easy to make in the Instant Pot. Dried figs take the flavor over the top!

INGREDIENTS

- 20 ounces canned coconut cream
- 1 packet yogurt starter culture
- 2 tablespoons gelatin
- 2 cups fresh or dried figs, chopped
- 1/2 cup maple syrup

COOKING STEPS

1. Add the coconut cream to the inner pot. Choose the "Yogurt" setting and bring it to a boil. Let it cool slightly (to 100 degrees F).

2. Now, add the yogurt starter culture; whisk to combine well. Program it back to the "Yogurt" function; let it pressure cook overnight. Use a natural release and carefully remove the lid.

3. Add the gelatin to the warm mixture. Pour the mixture into jars; top with the chopped figs and drizzle with maple syrup. Serve well chilled.

141. PEACH AND RASPBERRY CRUMBLE

 4 Servings

 Ready in about 20 minutes

PER SERVING:
286 Calories; 12.1g Fat; 42.8g Carbs; 4.4g Protein; 20.3g Sugars

If you have just found out that you can make great desserts in your Instant Pot, you probably feel great! Therefore, prepare an incredibly moist and tasty fruit crumble in 20 minutes and delight your family!

INGREDIENTS

- 2 peaches, pitted, peeled and cubed
- A pinch of freshly grated nutmeg
- A pinch of salt
- 1/4 teaspoon ground cloves
- 1 teaspoon ground cinnamon
- 1/2 teaspoon ground anise star
- 1 cup raspberries
- 1/2 cup water
- 1/4 cup date syrup
- 3 tablespoons coconut oil
- 1 cup old fashioned rolled oats
- 3 tablespoons all-purpose flour

COOKING STEPS

1. Lay the peaches on the bottom of your cooker. Sprinkle with all seasonings. Top with fresh raspberries.

2. Pour in the water. In a mixing dish, combine the other ingredients; whisk until everything is well incorporated. Add the mixture to the cooker.

3. Seal the cooker's lid and select the "Manual" setting. Set the machine to cook for 10 minutes under HIGH pressure.

4. Once cooking is complete, use a natural release. Allow it to cool slightly since the mixture will thicken as it sits. Eat warm with fresh whipped cream. Bon appétit!

142. NANA'S FAMOUS WALNUT FUDGE BROWNIES

 4 Servings

 Ready in about 25 minutes

PER SERVING:
499 Calories; 23.7g Fat; 73.3g Carbs; 5.3g Protein; 61.5g Sugars

Brownies at your fingertips! The Instant Pot turns regular brownies into a royally luxurious dessert. To make an old-fashioned version, don't forget to add the finely ground walnuts.

INGREDIENTS

- 3 ½ tablespoons butter
- 3 tablespoons chocolate chips
- 3/4 cup caster sugar
- 1 egg
- 1 egg yolk
- 1/2 teaspoon pure vanilla extract
- 1 teaspoon pure almond extract
- 1/2 cup cake flour
- 3 tablespoons baking cocoa
- 1/4 cup walnuts, ground

For the Frosting:

- 5 tablespoons butter, at room temperature
- 3 tablespoons cocoa powder
- 1 cup sugar, powdered
- A pinch of salt
- A pinch of grated nutmeg
- 4 tablespoons cream

COOKING STEPS

1. Firstly, melt the butter and chocolate chips in your microwave for 1 minute. Transfer to a mixing bowl.

2. Add the sugar, egg, egg yolk, vanilla and almond extract; mix to combine thoroughly. Now, add the flour, baking cocoa, and walnuts; mix again.

3. Prepare the Instant Pot by adding the water to the pot and placing the steam rack on top.

4. Line a baking dish with foil; now, lightly grease the foil using a nonstick cooking spray. Scrape the batter into the dish; lower the dish onto the rack.

5. Set your machine to cook for 16 minutes at HIGH pressure. Once cooking is complete, use a quick release and slowly remove the top. Let your brownies cool completely.

6. Meanwhile, make the frosting by mixing the butter and cocoa powder until smooth. Stir in the powdered sugar and mix well.

7. Add the salt, nutmeg, and cream; mix on medium-high until everything is well combined. Spread the prepared frosting onto the chilled brownies. Bon appétit!

Dessert Recipes | Instant Pot Cookbook

143. EXTRAVAGANT CURRANT RICE PUDDING

 4 Servings

 Ready in about 25 minutes

PER SERVING: 402 Calories; 4.8g Fat; 83.2g Carbs; 7.4g Protein; 41.8g Sugars

This simple and totally decadent rice pudding is a must-have for Sunday afternoon! Be sure to use a natural release to prevent the pudding from splattering.

INGREDIENTS

- 2 cups coconut milk
- 2 cups rice milk
- 2 cups water
- 3/4 cup jasmine rice
- 2 pared peels from a lemon
- 1/2 teaspoon grated nutmeg
- 1/4 teaspoon ground anise star
- 1 teaspoon cinnamon powder
- 1 cup brown sugar
- 1 egg yolk
- 1 teaspoon vanilla paste
- 1/2 cup currants

COOKING STEPS

1. Pour coconut milk, rice milk, and water into your Instant Pot; bring to a gentle boil. Add the rice, lemon peel, and spices. Give it a good stir.

2. Seal the lid and cook at HIGH pressure for 14 minutes. Once cooking is complete, use a natural release and carefully remove the lid according to the manufacturer's instructions.

3. Select "Sauté" mode and add the brown sugar, egg yolk, and vanilla paste. Once the mixture begins to boil, push the "Cancel" button.

4. Immediately fold in the currants and stir well. Serve warm or cold in individual bowls.

144. AROMATIC WINE-POACHED APPLES

 6 Servings

 Ready in about 25 minutes

PER SERVING:
376 Calories; 0.3g Fat; 73.6g Carbs; 0.9g Protein; 41.7g Sugars

If you are not in a hurry, soak the apples in their cooking liquid overnight; then, cook the sauce until it has thickened.

INGREDIENTS

- 1 bottle white wine
- 2 ½ cups water
- 1 ½ cups caster sugar
- 1/2 lemon, cut into rounds
- 2 cinnamon sticks
- 4-5 whole cloves
- 1 vanilla bean
- 6 medium sized apples, peeled

COOKING STEPS

1. Add the wine, water, and sugar to the Instant Pot; stir until dissolved. Add the remaining ingredients and gently stir to combine. Secure the lid.

2. Select "Manual" mode and cook at HIGH pressure for 5 minutes. Lastly, perform a quick release.

3. Using a slotted spoon, transfer the apples to a bowl. Select "Sauté" mode and cook the sauce until it has thickened and reduced by half. Drizzle the sauce over the reserved apples. Enjoy!

145. Luscious Key Blueberry Delight

 8 Servings

 Ready in about 20 minutes

PER SERVING:
203 Calories; 5.5g Fat; 40.7g Carbs; 1.2g Protein; 38.2g Sugars

This is an excellent and simple dessert that will definitely please a crowd.

INGREDIENTS

- 10 ounces fresh blueberries
- 1 ½ cups granulated sugar
- 1 heaping tablespoon lime zest
- 1 egg, well whisked
- 1 egg yolk, well whisked
- A pinch of salt
- 3 tablespoons butter, softened

COOKING STEPS

1. Simply place the blueberries, granulated sugar, and lime zest into the Instant Pot and stir to combine.

2. Seal the cooker's lid in place; set the machine to cook for 1 minute at HIGH pressure. Once cooking is complete, perform a natural pressure.

3. Now, slowly pour the hot lime mixture into the eggs; add a pinch of salt. Transfer the mixture to the cooker and click the "Sauté" key; whisk until the curd thickens slightly.

4. Press the "Cancel" button. Fold in softened butter and stir again. Cover with a plastic wrap and chill overnight. Serve chilled and enjoy!

146. DECADENT MINT CHEESECAKE

 8 Servings

 Ready in about 1 hour + chilling time

PER SERVING: 361 Calories; 19.8g Fat; 40.6g Carbs; 6.5g Protein; 28.3g Sugars

Make your cheesecake filling a little more excessive by adding fine chocolate mints. This is one of those desserts that taste better the second day.

INGREDIENTS

For the Crust:
- 1 cup gingersnap crumbs
- 1 teaspoon ground cinnamon
- 1/3 cup sugar
- 3 tablespoons butter

For the Filling:
- 1/2 pound cream cheese
- 1/2 cup sugar
- 2 eggs
- 1 teaspoon vanilla essence
- 2 tablespoons all-purpose flour
- 24 thin mints, crushed

COOKING STEPS

1. Prepare the cooker by adding the water to the inner pot and placing a steam rack on top.

2. Mix all ingredients for the crust; then, press the crust into a springform pan. Place in your refrigerator until it is ready to use.

3. Then, beat the cream cheese with sugar using an electric mixer until light and fluffy. Add the eggs and vanilla essence and beat until pale and creamy. Add the flour and beat again. Fold in 12 crushed mints.

4. Spread the filling onto the chilled crust. Now, lower the pan onto the rack. Then, select "Manual" mode; set your Instant pot to cook for 50 minutes at LOW pressure. Lastly, use a natural release and remove the lid according to the manual.

5. Let your cheesecake cool to room temperature; now, cover and refrigerate overnight before slicing and serving.

6. To serve, release your cake from the pan and decorate with remaining 12 mints. Bon appétit!

Dessert Recipes | Instant Pot Cookbook

147. EVERY-DAY BANANA BREAD MUFFINS

 8 Servings

 Ready in about 40 minutes

PER SERVING: 263 Calories; 10.0g Fat; 42.6g Carbs; 3.0g Protein; 25.3g Sugars

There are a zillion fantastic ideas for muffins; make these muffins instead of classic banana bread ones and indulge your sweet tooth! Keep this recipe in your back pocket.

INGREDIENTS

- 1 stick butter, softened
- 1 cup caster sugar
- 1 egg
- A pinch of nutmeg
- 1/2 teaspoon pure almond extract
- 1/2 teaspoon pure vanilla extract
- 1/4 teaspoon ground cloves
- 1 teaspoon cinnamon
- 2 large-sized ripe bananas, mashed
- 1 1/3 cups cake flour
- 1/2 teaspoon baking soda
- 1/2 teaspoon baking powder
- A pinch of salt
- 1/4 cup buttermilk

COOKING STEPS

1. In a mixing dish, beat the butter and sugar until creamy. Add the egg, nutmeg, almond extract, vanilla extract, ground cloves, and cinnamon; mix well.

2. Fold in mashed bananas and mix again.

3. In another mixing dish, thoroughly combine the flour, baking soda, and baking powder; add the salt and mix to combine.

4. Then, slowly stir this mixture into the egg mixture, while mixing continuously. Lastly, add the buttermilk mixture.

5. Prepare your Instant Pot by adding 2 cups of water and a stainless-steel trivet. Divide the mixture among mini silicone baking cups. Lower the cups onto the trivet.

6. Choose "Manual" mode and set your machine to cook for 28 minutes. Work in batches. When the machine beeps, use a natural release. To serve, top each muffin with a dollop of whipped

148. TRIPLE CHOCOLATE FUDGE CAKE

 8 Servings

 Ready in about 35 minutes

PER SERVING: 433 Calories; 23.7g Fat; 50.2g Carbs; 5.3g Protein; 43.2g Sugars

This fudge cake is an impressive dessert that is extra easy to make in the Instant Pot. Once you taste how good this cake is, it will become a staple for your holiday menu.

INGREDIENTS

For the Cake:
- 4 ounces high-quality milk chocolate, chopped
- 4 ounces dark chocolate, chopped
- 1 stick butter, room temperature
- 1/4 cup cocoa powder
- 1 cup confectioners' sugar
- 2 ½ tablespoons flour
- 1/4 teaspoon baking soda
- 2 eggs plus 1 egg yolk
- 1 teaspoon vanilla extract
- A pinch of kosher salt
- 1/4 teaspoon grated nutmeg
- 1/2 teaspoon ground cinnamon

For the Frosting:
- 1/2 stick butter
- 1/2 cup brown sugar
- 3 tablespoons whipping cream
- 1 cup powdered sugar
- 1/2 teaspoon pure almond extract
- 1/2 cup toasted hazelnuts, chopped

COOKING STEPS

1. In a microwave-safe bowl, melt both chocolates along with 1 stick of butter.

2. Add the rest of the above ingredients for the cake and mix to combine well. Then, lightly grease the bottom and sides of a springform pan. Scrape the mixture into the pan.

3. Prepare your Instant Pot by adding a steamer and 1 ½ cups of water to the bottom. Lower the pan onto the steamer and select "Manual" mode. Pressure cook for 8 minutes. Once cooking is complete, use a quick release.

4. Meanwhile, make the frosting. Heat a saucepan over a moderate flame. Then, add 1/2 stick of butter, brown sugar, and whipping cream; boil for 1 minute.

5. Remove from the heat and stir in the remaining ingredients; whisk to combine well. Cook for about 4 minutes, or until the frosting has thickened slightly. Pour immediately over the prepared cake.

149. ELEGANT CREAMY TROPICAL DESSERT

 6 Servings

 Ready in about 25 minutes

PER SERVING:
317 Calories; 6.5g Fat; 61.2g Carbs; 5.8g Protein; 32.2g Sugars

Rice pudding is very customizable and easy to make dessert! You can enjoy this silky and sophisticated dessert all year long.

INGREDIENTS

- 2 cups water
- 1 ½ cups milk
- 1 tablespoon brandy
- 1 cup short or medium grain rice
- A pinch of grated nutmeg
- A pinch of kosher salt
- 1/2 cup muscovado sugar
- 1 tablespoon maple syrup
- 1 whole egg, well-beaten
- 2 tablespoons butter
- 1/2 teaspoon vanilla extract
- 2 (2-inch) strips orange zest
- 1 tablespoon toasted coconut, shredded
- 1 papaya, skin removed, seeded and diced
- 1 pineapple, skin and core removed, diced

COOKING STEPS

1. Pour the water, milk, and brandy into your Instant Pot. Add the rice, nutmeg, salt, sugar, maple syrup, and the beaten egg; stir to combine well.

2. Next, select "Manual" mode; cook for 8 minutes at HIGH pressure. Now, use a natural release and carefully open the pot.

3. Add the butter, vanilla, orange zest, and toasted coconut; gently stir until everything is well incorporated. Serve topped with papaya and pineapple. Bon appétit!

150. BERRY AND PRUNE COMPOTE

 6 Servings

 Ready in about 30 minutes

PER SERVING:
224 Calories; 1.0g Fat; 57.0g Carbs; 2.4g Protein; 40.6g Sugars

There are so many ways to serve this delectable compote. Spoon it on top of your favorite ice cream; swirl into Greek-style yogurt; serve with pancakes. The possibilities are endless!

INGREDIENTS

- 1 pound fresh blueberries
- 1/2 pound fresh cranberries
- 1/4 pound fresh blackberries
- 1/2 cup prunes, pitted and chopped
- 1/3 cup sugar
- 2 tablespoons orange juice
- 2 cinnamon sticks
- 2 vanilla beans
- 4-6 whole cloves

COOKING STEPS

1. Place the fruits and sugar into the Instant Pot; stir to combine well.

2. Add the remaining ingredients and seal the lid. Cook at HIGH pressure for 8 minutes.

3. Once cooking is complete, use a natural release. Remove from heat; serve warm or chilled with vanilla ice cream.

Lisa Olson is an Austin-based food blogger and recipe developer who has attended the Auguste Escoffier School of Culinary Arts in Austin, Texas. She has now written several cookbooks, some of which are already up for sale on Amazon and more are on their way.

When she is not cooking in the kitchen you can usually find her wandering at the Barton Creek Farmers' Market or spending time at home with her two lovely little daughters, who also help her in the kitchen sometimes. Lisa Olson lives in Austin, Texas with her family and their dachshund Rocky.

With her books she wants to help you cook healthy and delicious meals for your family and make the process fun and easy, so you can really enjoy it.

You can visit her website: lisaolsoncooking.com

www.ingramcontent.com/pod-product-compliance
Lightning Source LLC
LaVergne TN
LVHW070948070426
835507LV00028B/3449